BBC MUSIC GUIDES

———

BEETHOVEN STRING QUARTETS 2

D1589532

BBC MUSIC GUIDES

General Editor: LIONEL SALTER

Bach Cantatas J. A. WESTRUP
Bach Organ Music PETER WILLIAMS
Bartók Orchestral Music JOHN MCCABE
Beethoven Concertos and Overtures ROGER FISKE
Beethoven Piano Sonatas DENIS MATTHEWS
Beethoven Symphonies ROBERT SIMPSON
Berlioz Orchestral Music HUGH MACDONALD
Brahms Chamber Music IVOR KEYS
Brahms Orchestral Music JOHN HORTON
Brahms Songs ERIC SAMS
Debussy Orchestral Music DAVID COX
Debussy Piano Music FRANK DAWES
Elgar Orchestral Music MICHAEL KENNEDY
Handel Concertos STANLEY SADIE
Haydn String Quartets ROSEMARY HUGHES
Haydn Symphonies H. C. ROBBINS LANDON
Mahler Symphonies and Songs PHILIP BARFORD
Mendelssohn Chamber Music JOHN HORTON
Monteverdi Madrigals DENIS ARNOLD
Mozart Chamber Music A. HYATT KING
Rachmaninov Orchestral Music PATRICK PIGGOTT
Ravel Orchestral Music LAURENCE DAVIES
Schoenberg Chamber Music ARNOLD WHITTALL
Schubert Chamber Music J. A. WESTRUP
Schubert Piano Sonatas PHILIP RADCLIFFE
Schubert Songs MAURICE J. E. BROWN
Schubert Symphonies MAURICE J. E. BROWN
Schumann Piano Music JOAN CHISSELL
Schumann Songs ASTRA DESMOND
Tchaikovsky Symphonies and Concertos JOHN WARRACK
Vaughan Williams Symphonies HUGH OTTAWAY

BBC MUSIC GUIDES

Beethoven String Quartets 2

BASIL LAM

BRITISH BROADCASTING CORPORATION

Contents

Published by the British Broadcasting Corporation
35 Marylebone High Street, London W1M 4AA
ISBN 0 563 12675 2
First published 1975
© Basil Lam 1975
Printed in England by The Whitefriars Press Ltd,
London and Tonbridge

Introduction

It is a commonplace which happens to be true that Beethoven developed, throughout his career, with a consistency scarcely to be paralleled in art. Goethe, for all his limited understanding of Beethoven's music, recognised the qualities in its creator that made this achievement possible when he wrote, after their first meeting in July 1812, 'Zusammengefasster, energischer, inniger, habe ich noch keinen Künstler gesehen'. ('Never have I met an artist more resolutely concentrated, more energetic, or of deeper sincerity'.)

Some composers have never surpassed the finest works of their first maturity (Handel, Brahms); others have improved beyond reasonable expectation in style and feeling (Verdi, Wagner), but what is unique to Beethoven is the unhurried, calm (Gefasst) progression, in so many genres, from perfect early works to not less perfect deeper ones which never invalidate or supersede their predecessors. The late quartets, obviously 'greater' than the Op. 18s and the Rasumovskys, are not more unmistakably the creations of a supreme master of composition. Eliot reminded us – with specific reference to Shakespeare – that the life-work of certain great artists should be considered as a unity; the splendour (Herrlichkeit) and veracity (Wahrheit) intuitively recognised in the Beethoven of 1812 by Bettina Brentano are to be found in the piano trios Op. 1, as in the C sharp minor quartet he thought his greatest work.

With Op. 74 the harmonic amplitude, the grand instrumental rhetoric of the Op. 59 quartets, is taken to the stage beyond which breadth would have verged on diffuseness. It was finished in the summer of 1809, Beethoven's 'E flat' year when he also produced the 'Emperor' concerto and the 'Les Adieux' sonata. The next quartet could scarcely have been more different in all except the authentic stamp of greatness.

Op. 95 in F minor

Op. 95 is sometimes called a transitional work, but if this epithet has a meaning it must carry the implication of diverse elements not perfectly integrated. This may be said of Op. 74 (see Beethoven

String Quartets Vol. 1, pp. 64–8), but its successor of 1810, the bitter fruit of a barren year, belongs neither with the earlier quartets nor with those of Beethoven's final maturity. The designation on the autograph, 'Quartett[o] Serioso', is as strange as the work itself, which could hardly be considered frivolous; did Beethoven in a mood of angry disillusion regard the previous quartets as too brilliant to satisfy him?

To compare this quartet with that earlier F minor tragedy, the 'Appassionata', is to recognise in the piano work an element of expansive rhetoric that might well seem inadequate to the Beethoven of 1810; but his renunciation of spacious harmonic structures was not permanent, and within a year he was sketching the Seventh Symphony. Any attempt to relate a composer's work to what is known of his life is bound to be a crude over-simplification, if only because music has a complex life of its own that resists verbalisation; but a style in which ideas expand in cumulative rhythmic patterns reflects a state of mind in which it is possible, in Eliot's phrase, to construct something upon which to rejoice. On 2 May 1810 Beethoven, in a letter to his old friend Wegeler, wrote:

If I had not read somewhere that no one should quit life voluntarily while he could still do something worth while, I would have been dead long ago and certainly by my own hand. Oh, life is so beautiful, but for me it is poisoned for ever.

This Werther-like mood did not last, and he was pleasantly distracted by Bettina Brentano; but on 9 July he wrote to Nikolaus Zmeskall, the dedicatee of Op. 95 and perhaps his most intimate Viennese friend, 'Sometimes I feel as though I might go mad because of my undeserved fame'.

The man who had made the proud resolution not to conceal his deafness was again oppressed by the 'demon in his ears', and it was not until the autumn that he could concentrate on a major work. The autograph of Op. 95 says 'written in the month of October', and the sketches run consecutively. Before assuming, however, that this sombre masterpiece is a transcript from life we must note that the far from tragic 'Archduke' Trio was also coming into being at this time of disappointment and anger, a reminder that Beethoven's music is no more to be taken as autobiographical than is the work of Haydn or Mozart.

The whole first movement of Op. 95 is scarcely longer than the development alone in that of Op. 59 no. 1; if its brevity were the result of a process of 'miniaturisation' it would merely be small, a sonatina for strings. The peculiarity of its greatness is that the elements are compressed as though by a more than gravitational force of the mind, so that the impression of magnitude is strengthened. The opening two-bar unison, for example, is followed by the three bars of formal tonic-dominant in dotted rhythm. As in Op. 57 and Op. 59 no. 2, a sequential repetition of the opening begins on the flat supertonic, to vanish into sustained harmony restating the dominant. The rapid motion of the first bars is continued in the Bruckner-like cello figure, then by the reiteration in the viola's deepest register of the five notes that are to dominate the whole movement. Now the main theme can expand in a real counterstatement, the bare octaves sounding grimly powerful after the fully-scored bars 6–17; and when harmony is resumed no transition is needed to establish D flat for the second subject, led by the viola. In a few bars this establishes a Wagnerian breadth of harmonic motion into which the pervasive four-semiquaver figure is soon absorbed. Astonishingly, the exposition finds space to repeat the closing section of the second group.

In terms of conventional analysis, what follows is a development leading to a recapitulation in which the beginning of the first subject is omitted, but Beethoven, unlike some of his critics, is not the slave of terminology, and such an account does not represent the true course of events. If we must use this descriptive language, a more accurate formulation would be that the exposition leads directly to a modified recapitulation, beginning in the tonic major, in which the first group is greatly expanded, thus obviating the need for any development section at all. No unexpected turn to a remote key could equal the force of the tonic major (bar 60) after the prolonged pianissimo D flat at the close of the exposition. The structural principle of sonata form is tonality, not contrast of themes; this so-called development never moves away from F as key-centre and contains the only return of the dotted rhythm of bars 3–5. By dispensing with a development Beethoven is able to keep the whole movement within a range of key more closely circumscribed than in any other important classical sonata movement. After the tremendous impact of F major (cf. Op. 57, first movement, bars 151-2 ff.) the minor returns until the expanded second subject moves, with no less wonderful effect, from D flat to the home tonic. The rest of this recapitulation, including the repetition (with one startling change in the upward scale) of the closing section seems to establish F major as if to say 'Plus fait douceur que violence'. Both in exposition and recapitulation D flat has been the key of a calm and noble pathos (as in the 'Appassionata'), and tragic irony is at its most telling when the coda brings back the main theme in this key, exactly reversing the harmonic process at the end of the exposition and banishing any hope of a happy ending for this brief tragedy in one act.

Thematic links between movements are rare in Beethoven, but the profoundly impressive four-bar opening of the D major *Allegretto* is subtly related to the first movement theme, as may be seen by a transposed quotation:

Ex. 1

I. Allegro con brio

II. Allegretto ma non troppo

As the *Allegretto* is joined to the *Allegro* that follows it, the separation of the finale by its slow introduction from the preceding three movements is further emphasised by this appearance in the *Allegretto* of a theme related to the first movement.

Nottebohm remarks that in the 1810 sketchbook containing Op. 95 Beethoven wrote out various passages from Bach's *Chromatic Fantasia and Fugue,* and it seems reasonable to relate this fact to the persistent chromaticism of the quartet's slow movement. The expressive chromatic inflections of Mozart's melodic style are found only in early Beethoven, being as foreign to his own type of theme as was chromatic harmony to his structural methods when he began to compose large works. In this *Allegretto* the principal section, in contrast with the fugue that follows, has a subtle ambiguity of key produced by the use of alternative forms of degrees of the scale, which is not the same thing as normal chromaticism, but leads to harmonies of uncommon sensitivity, poised between major and minor at any chosen moment, yet always clearly belonging to the former. Thus in the first eight-bar phrase, closing in the dominant, the four notes G, B, C, and D all appear in two forms: G, G♯; B, B♭; C♯, C♮; D, D♯; but only a single B♭′ inflects the D major of the melody. Except for the strangely harsh cadences, darkened by shadowy diminished sevenths, the broad theme moves into an unclouded D major.

The central fugue section, on a subject distantly related to the cello phrase in the first bars, is nearer to Bach than to anything in Beethoven's own music. Besides the '48' and the *Art of Fugue* he possessed Kirnberger's works, which contain solutions to the very chromatic canons in the *Musical Offering*. Before this fugue, as haunting and mysterious as the one in G sharp minor ('48', Book II), proceeds to a second section, the opening phrase of the movement is developed as an episode in sequential steps beneath sustained harmonies reminiscent, as Hans Gal once pointed out, of Mozart's introduction to his 'Dissonance' Quartet, K.465. The second fugue, with its inversion of the subject (viola, bars 87ff.) and weird counter-subject, eludes definition. Eventually the upbeat figure of the subject becomes a tritone in conflict with its inversion as perfect fifth (see bars 93–110), and the strain on classical tonality anticipates the music of the late nineteenth century. Towards the end of the movement the opening few notes of the fugue subject return to cast a shadow across the reprise, and in the very last bars the derivation of this theme from the opening bars is made plain.

Ex. 2
bars184 ff.
[Allegro ma non troppo]

As the quotation shows, the movement could end in peace, but D major is replaced by a diminished seventh, from which the third movement begins. Beauty is not the aim of this notable manifestation of controlled rage, which is made out of the barest elements possible: a three-note figure and a scale, both inverted when required and both in jagged dotted rhythm. Beethoven's ripest mastery is evident in the distinction between the two figures

♪♩. ♪ and ♪♩♪♩♪♩

Note the two appearances, in the deceptively calm 'trio', of the D major tonality of the *Allegretto*. The quicker tempo for the second reprise of the principal section is a drastic resource used, in milder context, for the minuet of Op. 18 no. 4. In Op. 95 the curtailment of this reprise (the first sixteen bars are omitted) enhances the forbidding abruptness of the last unison phrase – *Coriolanus* again or Haydn's 'Great Mogul'.

To compare the final sonata-rondo and its introduction with the 'Malinconia' and finale of Op. 18 no. 6 is to realise how far Beethoven's art had developed in the decade between, though the earlier work is no less true to experience. The Beethoven of 1800 could exorcise 'loathed melancholy' by the very enjoyment of his ability to express it (like Keats in his Ode), together with a very normal and healthy self-regard. It is a mark of unusual sensibility to be as melancholy as this. In Op. 95 all that is permitted is a brief tender rebuke to the arrogant assertiveness of the previous movement: commentators should not exaggerate the note of yearning in the sensitively harmonised leading-note of the dominant in the sixth and seventh bars; Beethoven is not a very Tristan-like character.

The finale can no more adopt a tone of strenuous triumph than can Mozart's in his G minor Quintet, after its awe-inspiring tragic prelude, but where the earlier work over-reacts into a slightly facile pathetic gaiety, Beethoven finds a perfect conclusion to his quartet, too heartfelt for cynicism, too light in rhythm and texture for the tense smile of the professional stoic. He had already written, in the piano sonata Op. 31 no. 2, a finale with something of the same undemonstrative fortitude in adversity, but whereas the sonata movement moved with such Bach-like uniformity that it could simply end within a phrase-length, the quartet has traversed a vastly wider range of experience and demands a peroration. What it gets is a comic-opera coda, absurdly and deliberately unrelated to this 'quartett serioso', the Shakespearian touch that provides the final confirmation of the truth of the rest.

Op. 127 in E flat major

During the twelve years between Op. 95 and the first sketches for Op. 127 Beethoven endured long periods of artistic as well as personal frustration. Though these years saw the composition of the six piano sonatas from Op. 90 (1814) to Op. 111 (1821–2) and the near-completion of the *Missa Solemnis,* the slowing of his creative activity was so marked that between August 1814 and the spring of 1819 he wrote only five major works: the two cello sonatas Op. 102, the piano sonatas Opp. 101 and 106, and the song-cycle *An die ferne Geliebte.*

He returned to the string quartet after relinquishing the public domain with the great Mass and the last symphony, and after that stupendous 'farewell to the piano', the Diabelli Variations. It is important to realise, however, that these five incomparable masterpieces of chamber music were not Beethoven's intended 'last message' to the world. His untimely death came at a point when he was full of new ideas for such things as a Tenth Symphony, a Requiem and a string quintet. The impression of finality is due to the universal acknowledgement of the quartets as the *summa* of instrumental music. The contrast with Bach is not to be resisted; whereas Bach by the age of fifty-five, having exhausted the expressive powers of music as he knew it, sought consolation in the complexities of formal abstraction, Beethoven, whose barren years had come earlier, experienced a renewal of activity after which he could say in a notable meiosis (apropos of Op. 131), 'Thank God there is less lack [of invention/fantasy] than before'.

In the *Missa Solemnis* and the Ninth Symphony the resources of music as a communicating art were strained to the verge of impossibility; perfection became not so much unattainable as irrelevant to Beethoven's ethical passion for the Just City. Because he turned away from the populous world to write his latest works in a more than Miltonic isolation, it is often assumed that he moved into an ever more concentrated subjectivity. The converse may be nearer the truth. The Mass and the symphony are the utterances of a man speaking to men, but in the last quartets Beethoven is as indifferent to communication as to self-expression. It may be objected that the first movement of Op. 132 expresses suffering, anxiety, pain, and that such were terribly present in Beethoven's life, or that (according to Holz) he himself spoke of his sense of overwhelming grief when he wrote the Cavatina of Op. 130. Conceding this, one must then ask where in his secular existence were the sources of the variations in Op. 127, the Scherzo of Op. 131, the *Alla tedesca* of Op. 130. . . . Who would attempt to relate the B minor Mass to the stolid provincialism of Bach's life as Cantor of St Thomas's?

Op. 127 has always been considered the most 'normal' of the five quartets and has therefore escaped the attentions of those musical philosophers who have soared into the 'intense inane' in their attempts to elucidate the meaning of the middle three of the five. Its greatness is beyond question, but the simplification of the idea apparent in the last three piano sonatas (compare Op. 111 with Op. 106) is continued to such a degree that the difficulty of comprehension is to come to terms not so much with extreme complexity as with a blinding simplicity. We are faced with this in the opening bars, an introduction which both here and in its two reappearances would surely have seemed impossibly naïve (in harmony, not rhythm) to the composer of the 'Malinconia' in Op. 18 no. 6, the *Andante* at the beginning of Op. 59 no. 3, or the *Poco adagio* of Op. 74. These three are full of invention, personal, in fact, where the later Beethoven seems to discover what already exists, a Newton organising the concepts that make the universe of music understandable. So with the *Allegro* of Op. 127; themes are not contrasted but drawn together; the dramatic events that in earlier works mark the main transitions of sonata form are deliberately obscured, so that the two returns of the *maestoso*, in G and C, become crucial to the overall structure. I have suggested that Beethoven came to regard almost every melodic elaboration, even in a theme, as a variation for which the source must be found. This *Allegro* provides a wonderful example. Ex. 3 shows the first theme (treble and bass only). With its self-repeating three bars making an eight-bar phrase this could scarcely be simpler, but when it is 'developed' (bars 81ff.) the first violin introduces, bars 89ff., a descending tetrachord, given prominence by reinforcing octaves on the third beat, and this ancient figure (one of the Renaissance archetypal ground basses – see the *minore* trio section in the third movement of Op. 18 no. 3) becomes increasingly significant (Ex. 4.)

What is its origin here?

The first theme can be seen as a variation of it:

and it is also evident in the second (bars 41ff.). In the development the tetrachord is associated with sequences built on the melodic fourths of the main theme (and of the *maestoso*) and so is absent when other material is being discussed. Its entries are bars 89 (first violin), 99 (viola), 103 (cello), 117 (first violin and viola). It then vanishes; even its reflection in the bass in the first bars of the *Allegro* fails to reappear in the recapitulation, so carefully united in a seamless join with the development. (Compare bars 167ff. with bars 7ff.) Confidence in the eventual reappearance of what Beethoven so deliberately brought to the foreground should not distract from awareness of the return in the tonic major of the second-subject melody that, with a hint of plaintiveness, had first been in G minor. The recapitulation thus dispels even that shadow of darker moods, and its formal close on tonic chords leads to the subdominant; evidently there is to be a coda. The tetrachord now returns merged with its other form in the bass of the first four bars of the *Allegro*, and broadens with overlapping entries in a polyphony as plain and as miraculously felicitous as the most inspired creations of Josquin three centuries earlier. The first violin's ascent to the heights as the coda moves towards its quiet close gives a real presence to what in the last piano sonatas could only be imagined.

The suggestion that Beethoven's latest style evolved through simplification might seem to be invalidated by the growing prominence of variations in the music of his last years, but the themes out of which these variations grow are themselves precisely those final simplicities, purified of all expressive alloy.

Variation as a technique for extending musical ideas brings with it basic problems of aesthetics, and where the theme is itself a statement as deep as it is complete the process of making variations on it must be called in question. In the two greatest independent sets of variations, the Goldberg and the Diabelli, the problem does not appear, as in the one the theme is a bass and a harmonic scheme, in the other it is a sturdy prosaic structure of no emotional significance. Before the Viennese classics the same precarious validity is shown in the da capo aria, where the compulsory decorations of the reprise are tolerable only when the theme is of a secondary order of inspiration.

In Op. 127, the numerous sketches for the slow movement theme make a strange sequence quite unlike the continuous process, generally attributed to Beethoven, of perfecting a rough outline. The very first sketch gives the opening bar of the great melody, then pages of useless variants follow before the phrase can be completed. All this is not so much invention as the clarifying of vision, so that something already known can be realised in notation.

The *Adagio* of Op. 59 no. 2 (*Si tratta questo pezzo con molto di sentimento*) expresses a mood of contemplation; this theme is the object of contemplation, no more concerned with expression or communication than is a Gothic interior that evokes a response by its perfection of order, harmony and remoteness from common experience. If the perfection of the theme is conceded, how can it be submitted to variation? If we accept the classical definition of perfection its integrity can only be marred by alteration, but the whole movement maintains the level of its beginning, and contrary to universal procedure the first variation is the most complex of the set. A building, a statue, a painting exists outside time, to which, as Leonardo unkindly observed, music is inescapably subject; the theme, in its unworldly calm, is as nearly timeless as music can be, and the difficulties mentioned vanish with the realisation that the variations are expressive of the various responses of the awakened imagination to the experience of contemplating the theme itself. The melody emerges, as from a vast distance, over a pedal that becomes explicit (as a dominant seventh) only on the last quaver, the bass moving to the A flat chord *after* the melody, and instead of ending, the last phrase merges into a brief coda, wonderfully expressive in its warm harmonies through which the vision is withdrawn. The first variation, while faithful to the structure of the theme, dwells joyfully on some of its melodic phrases, infused with chromatic inflections so harmonised as to exclude pathos. The codetta, not being part of the theme, is in its varied form here even more beautiful than before.

A heavenly levity pervades the *Andante con moto*, with its naïve serenade-like accompaniment to the fantastically elaborate duet of the two violins; nothing like this had been heard since the 'Domine Deus' of the B minor Mass.

Beethoven's *In dulci jubilo*, though it sounds completely spontaneous, is a true variation, not a free fantasia. Ex. 6, overleaf, shows the theme in the first phrase. With the change of key to the flat submediant (F flat written as E; there is nothing enharmonic here) we are brought back to the human world of aspiration and prayer. Significantly, Beethoven's 'cantabile', always reserved for the inexpressive sublime, is now replaced by 'molto espressivo', with wide

Ex. 6

melodic intervals and highly charged harmony. Bruckner was surely inspired by this variation in the profound *Adagio* of his Sixth Symphony, and the possibility of such an association is indicative of its remoteness from the rest of the quartet.

The structure of the theme is more closely followed than elsewhere in the movement, with cello and violin alternating phrase by phrase. In the second half (note that the wonderful compression of the melody earns the marking *cantabile*) the extreme height to which the cello ascends produces a climax of an intensity not to be long endured, that fades through a chromatically weakened cadence (representing the original codetta) resolving on to a unison. F flat drops a semitone to the dominant of the home key and the last complete variation begins, in a texture very like that of the theme; the cello statement of the first phrase is marked *cantabile* and the change of rhythm from ♩ ♪ to ♩ ♫ is the only element of variation. The second section had, in its repetition, touched on the dominant seventh of the dominant (bar 17 into 18), but now this becomes a real harmonic change, inexplicably radiant and transfiguring the melody.

The original cadence has not been heard since the end of the theme. Now it returns in the bass, then echoed with subdominant harmony leading to the central mystery of the whole work, in twelve bars of austere polyphony based, not on the theme, but on the first articulate phrase that emerged from silence before it began. Tonally this belongs to the sub-dominant minor (C sharp for D flat) but when it moves towards A major this Neapolitan chord (B♭♭) in A flat turns quietly home to begin a variation in decorative melody as great as Bach's. It is considerably shorter than the theme and obviously cannot conclude a design containing a range of contrasts beyond the scope of any previous slow movement. What remains to be expanded to balance this last compression of the melody on which the whole has been constructed? Before reaching its formal close in the simplest possible cadence formula (bar 20) the codetta breaks off on a dominant seventh, and after a pause – the only silence in the piece – the repeated quavers that followed the E major variation are resumed with a *Zauberflöte* solemnity over the three notes of the original cadence bar, first A flat, B double flat, A flat; then, as at first, after another silence this elementary formula states the key of the supplicatory *Adagio* but no more, and the last bar dwells, *ritardando,* on a variation of the phrase that led into the theme.

The most commonplace formula of tonic and dominant chords having been glorified in the slow movement, a second such makes an enchantingly witty introduction to the scherzo, but it looks back, not forward; and this is its only appearance. In earlier works Beethoven could, by sheer force of character, make a convincing unity out of violent contrasts, following a serene *Adagio* by a powerfully humorous scherzo or a triumphant finale. In Op. 127 self-expression is superseded by a totally integrated vision in which contrasts are aspects of a neutral apprehension of reality, beyond the tensions and aggressions of mundane experience. So the movement that follows the theme and variations must renew activity, without merely reacting against the passivity of contemplation as though offering an alternative mode of response to experience. The *Scherzando vivace* has been likened to the *Allegretto vivace e sempre scherzando* of Op. 59 no. 1, but the resemblance is superficial. The earlier piece, splendidly wilful in the extremity of its contrasts, convinces by expressing the personality of its composer, but the Beethoven of 1825 is no more concerned with self-expression than was the Bach of the Goldberg Variations, where the same sense of intellectual joy comes from the awareness of a freedom so absolute that it can create its own limitations for the pure pleasure of transcending them.

So this movement in Op. 127 can invert its opening phrase, not with serious intent but to provide the alternative cadential figures that run through the piece, the hint of strenuous action in Ex. 7a being countered by its gently insistent opposite:

Ex. 7(a)

Even the fortissimo unisons in bars 36–40 are without cumulative emphasis, and when later (bars 60ff.) the persistent dotted rhythm, now in four-part harmony, threatens defiance this unacceptable intrusion is rebuked by the inexplicably droll *recitativo ma in tempo* of viola and cello.

The trio section, by making very long phrases over its reiterated accompanying crotchets, brings a relaxed ease (for the listener!) to the kind of texture generally used for onward-driving sequences in four-bar sections. Its key scheme is simple but effective. E flat minor, alternating with D flat and G flat for the strongly contrasted second theme 'im Volkston', leads eventually to the first solid appearance in the work of the home dominant (in the first movement the second group had avoided this area) and so to the reprise.

The theme of the finale, after its introductory unison, faintly reminiscent of the 'Eroica', makes an eight-bar phrase closing on the dominant, but the effect is of great rhythmic subtlety, matched by the no less unconventional harmony, in which the most ordinary diatonic processes are made to assume strange shapes. The 'foreign' A natural is a consequence of the first phrase in the scherzo (bar 5) – not that this makes it any less subversive of decorum. Attempts to find connections in melodic outline between this theme and that of the first movement may obscure the pleasing fact that both have the same structure, a repeated phrase with a full close only at the end. This applies to both themes of the first group (see bars 21–8).

The finale, though, has something of the second-period harmonic breadth, making possible a quite extensive 'false reprise' in the sub-dominant (bar 145), where the viola has the theme as bass in three-part writing as transparent as Mozart's. The gentle dismissal of this 'wrong' key for the true recapitulation in the tonic is ethereal enough for the variations of the second movement, and exquisite in tone-colour. The expected full close in A flat is evaded in bar 176, and the first violin begins one of the Pastoral Symphony-type se-quential repetitions of a single figure characteristic of the work. Beneath it thirds with displaced accents rise steadily until the tonic is reached (in its first inversion) and with it the first theme wonder-fully reharmonised; even the rough A♮' in the third bar is drawn into the surrounding euphony.

When the end of the recapitulation reaches a possible C minor, turning to major and fading in a *ritardando*, the expected modula-tion is surely to F minor, especially with the G''/A♭'' trill on the top of the C major chord. The change to the A♮'' is all that is needed to bring back the main theme in a new time (6/8), C major being the starting-point of a modulating sequence of which every magical change of key is brought about by that seemingly crude A♮

Ex. 8

When E flat is regained, the deaf master's imagination invents a quartet-texture quite unlike anything he or anyone else had ever heard; after the viola has given the two-bar summary of the theme a tonic pedal begins to resonate, and the rest of the coda, summing up the contrasts of the work, alternates between 'Eroica' Symphony grandeur and quiet lyricism. The crescendo at the very end underlines in red the leading note of the dominant (the notorious A natural), and there is no seventh (A flat) in the penultimate chord.

Op. 132 in A minor

Beethoven was occupied with Op. 132 before completing Op. 127, but the remoteness from classical tradition of the quartets in A minor, B flat and C sharp minor has led many commentators to regard them as an interrelated group, a triptych separated from Op. 127 and from Op. 135, which happened to be his last complete composition. Nottebohm remarked on the derivation of the *Grosse Fuge* subject from the opening of Op. 132, and enthusiasts for theories of thematic unity have seized eagerly on the further metamorphoses of this motif in Op. 131 and of course elsewhere in Op. 130. Perhaps its source is Bach's G minor Fugue ('48', Bk. I):

Ex. 9

These facts, though interesting as evidence of Beethoven's working methods, do little more than exemplify the scarcely surprising truth that a composer who, as he said on various occasions, liked to occupy himself with several compositions at the same time, explored diverse aspects of a basic note-set that happened to interest him during these last few years of his life.

There is no evidence of any kind to suggest that these three quartets were considered by Beethoven to be connected or related, and the listener's awareness of the integrity of any one of them can only be confused by the suggestion that thematic coincidences of identity imply relatedness of the works themselves.

What does constitute a genuine unity is Beethoven's whole creative life, in which certain fundamental 'ideas' may be traced in sequences of works from his earliest years to the unsurpassable achievements of final maturity. From this point of view Op. 127 can be seen as the culmination of a series of purely classical, objective sonata compositions in which personal expression is completely absorbed by the joyful play of the creative imagination. This would include (to name only works in E flat) the trios Op 1 no. 1 and Op. 3, the sonata Op. 31 no. 3, the so-called 'Emperor' concerto, and the trio Op. 70 no. 2. The A minor Quartet is at once the most remote and the most retrospective of Beethoven's latest works; after the marvellous 'final simplifications' of musical thought in Op. 127 the return to tragic and pathetic utterance involves a return to the language of another group of works, essentially the famous C minor–F minor sequence – though such critical categorisations, it must be remembered, are invented by critics. Beethoven's most tragic works are made finally exhilarating by the presence of the element Yeats found in Shakespeare when he wrote:

> All perform their tragic play,
> There struts Hamlet, there is Lear,
> That's Ophelia, that Cordelia;
> Yet they, should the last scene be there,
> The great stage curtain about to drop,
> If worthy their prominent part in the play,
> Do not break up their lines to weep.
> They know that Hamlet and Lear are gay;
> Gaiety transfiguring all that dread.[1]

The first movement of Op. 132 – it is a work of extremes – is full of unresolved tensions; unlike any of Beethoven's other tragedies it brings a sense of oppressiveness, being as sombre as the beginning of Op. 95, with neither the grand rage nor the lyrical ardour of that splendid outburst. It would be unseemly to vex his ghost

[1] W. B. Yeats, 'Lapis Lazuli', *Last Poems and Plays* (London 1940).

with pity, but for once the music here speaks of pain endured without the mitigation of hope or indignation.

The profound darkness of the sustained opening is not mysterious or indeed introductory, being in both respects quite unlike the beginning of Op. 59 no. 3. These eight *sostenuto* bars state the specific theme which is also the thematic type of the whole movement. Both in *rectus* and *inversus* the four-note motif encloses a fifth, but the possibilities of expansion contained in this interval are denied from the very beginning by the rhythm which stresses the notes that press inwards on the accented beats.

The *Allegro* converts these semitones into the appoggiaturas that Beethoven had progressively discarded as his style developed after the 1790s, but with the subtlety of final mastery he varies the context in which these highly expressive inflections are placed. Some appear in their traditional form (bars 13–14), others are so harmonised as to minimise the harmonic debilitation caused by an excess of appoggiaturas (as, for instance, in C.P.E. Bach or Wagner). The connection with Beethoven's early style and the degree to which it could inspire his deepest and most mature thought may be seen by setting the theme of this movement against that of Op. 18 no. 4.

Ex. 10(a)

Op. 132, I, bars 13 ff.
Allegro

(b)

Op. 18 no. 4
Allegro ma non tanto

In the later work what appears to be the main subject is perhaps better understood as a counter-subject to the four-note theme whose sibylline impressiveness pervades the movement. Though polyphony, as in all true quartet styles, is not rigorously maintained, this 'dark saying' controls the music almost as decisively as Bach's theme in the great C sharp minor fugue ('48', Book I, no. 4). Formal analysis readily identifies a 'second subject' in F major, but this forlorn lyrical fragment is unable to assert itself; it is little more than a variant of the first subject and its fragile identity is purely melodic, disturbed rather than supported by the strange restless accompaniment in broken triplets. The emotional strain characteristic of this movement shows itself in the extreme contrast – almost a conflict of styles – between the opening and the continuation of the F major section in a bland polyphony that would scarcely seem out of place in a work of the 1790s. The failure of the strength that is to be renewed in the slow movement is movingly expressed in the thrice-heard 'soft' cadence on the dominant of F major.

Ex. 11

To regard what follows as 'development' is to miss the point. The return of the four-semibreve 'motto' is so impressive as to banish all other elements, and it is at this stage that we realise that the 'first subject' is a counterpoint to the ineluctable theme that motivates the whole tragedy. Even the seemingly irrelevant new motif that appears in canon at bar 92 is derived from it, though this quasi-vocal utterance is also a reminiscence of the 1805 *Leonore* (the passage was deleted in the *Fidelio* revision)—Ex. 12 overleaf. But there is no escape, and the motto, fortissimo in E minor, brings with it the material of the exposition, though not until the inverted dominant pedal of this new key has established it as real (the sustained high B'' in bars 114–17). Note also the solid dominant instead of premature tonic chord on the upbeat (bars 10 and 120). Thematically all this is recapitulation; but the sonata-principle, flexible though it is, cannot survive the dislocation of tonal balance

Ex. 12 (a)

bars 92 ff.
Op. 132, I

(b)

Leonore, Act III, No. 17 (1805 version)
[Adagio]

FLORESTAN: O Le-o—no-re! Le-o—no-re!

involved in a reprise where neither first nor second group is in the home tonic. The latter, of course, is now in the C major of the canonic episode, and this return to the mediant of the main tonic emphasises the mood of passive suffering that Yeats considered unfit to be a subject for poetry. We are far from the Beethoven world of heroic conflict with its outward-directed harmonic expansions.

The pathetic cadence quoted is now in C major; it leads, after some hesitation, to A minor, where the main theme returns yet again. The second subject duly follows in A major, with an effect of tragic irony reminiscent of the D major horn solo just before the catastrophic end of the first movement in the Ninth Symphony. Here there is no possibility of a grand climax in the coda and the end is terribly abrupt, a desperate rallying of force like Florestan's feverish vision in his dungeon.

For Beethoven, life in the country meant something far deeper than the 'simple life'. A note among the sketches for the 'Hammerklavier' Sonata (1817–18) runs: 'Ein kleines Haus allda so klein, dass man allein nur ein wenig Raum hat ... nur einige Täge in dieser göttl[ichen] Briel ... Sehnsucht od[er] Verlange, Befreiung oder

Erfüllung'. ('A small house there, so small that one has only a little space . . . only a few days in this heavenly Brühl. Longing or yearning, liberation or fulfilment') .

So, after the oppressed first movement of Op. 132, ruled as sternly as any fugue by its grim four-note motif, the contrast had to be an evocation of rural peace and simplicity. Even as late as the sketching of the 'Heiliger Dankgesang' he wrote, as equivalent for scherzo, the piece that later became (in G instead of A) the *Alla danza tedesca* of Op. 130. In the final version of Op. 132 (the earlier work) this pastoral element finds its place in the trio section and includes another allemande (*tedesca*) written many years earlier.

The motive for this change of plan is not hard to discern; following immediately on the harsh ending of the *Allegro,* the exquisite evocation of a more than Virgilian Arcadia would seem merely dreamlike and, so, unreal. What actually follows is not an answer but a turning aside into purely musical fantasy – a whole piece made out of the double theme contained within two bars.

Ex. 13

Both in metrics and in tonality this ghost of the Mozartian *menuetto* remains subdued, without contrasts, without climax, revolving in sometimes dissonant combinations of the two subjects quoted. Nothing else in Beethoven is so like Brahms in his moods of grey Northern gloom, though there is nothing of the Brahmsian pathos. After this uncommunicative study in thematic concentration the rustic trio brings a deeply moving sense of renewed awareness and acceptance of the ordinary human world. Evocations of the musette or of the zampogna (bagpipe) were fashionable in the Baroque era, but often with an element of patronage. Beethoven knew, in Handel's Pastoral Symphony (*Messiah*), a pure example of the most poetic use of this convention, and the ethereal melody over its long drone bass in Op. 132 is no less wonderful than the trio section in the scherzo of the Ninth Symphony. The harmony, free from the least trace of antiquarian scrupulosity but quite unclassical (there is not a single G sharp in the principal refrain), prepares the ear for the modal slow movement. The Ländler that forms a middle section within the trio quotes from a work still earlier than the allemande already mentioned; the theme divided between viola and violin (bars 141ff.) comes straight from the *Largo* of the piano trio Op. 1 no. 2.

The contrast between 'scherzo' and trio sections is perhaps no more extreme than that between the tragic *Menuetto* of Mozart's D minor Quartet (K.421) and its trio with solo violin and pizzicato accompaniment, but the framing of the mundane little allemandes with the deeply poetic 'Pastorale' introduces a further and surely deliberate clash of style. For once Beethoven allows an extra-musical, even autobiographical motive to determine a musical scheme; and it is worth remembering, when the viola has a long solo (bars 149–73), that Beethoven played the viola in the Bonn Court orchestra during the years 1788–92. Such considerations are marginal; I suggest merely that the personal, even private references contained in the quotations were the source of this startling *collage,* a notable anticipation of twentieth-century technique.

Unlike Handel, who dismissed with Augustan confidence a polite suggestion that he might enlarge the resources of music by reviving the ancient modes, Beethoven was interested in earlier styles, reminding himself to 'study the hymns of the monks' for models of prosody and even copying into his sketch-books phrases of Palestrina. In 1820, while working on the *Missa Solemnis,* he almost certainly resorted to Glareanus's *Dodecachordon,* of which, as Martin Cooper has reminded us, the Lobkowitz library possessed a copy. His immediate concern was presumably with the Dorian modality of the 'Incarnatus', though we need not suppose he sought information on Glareanus's remarks that the Lydian mode was little used, as the 'correction' of the tritone F-B to F-B flat turned it into Ionian transposed. By writing his 'sacred song of thanksgiving' in strict Lydian Beethoven made the most extreme possible contrast with classical tonality: he himself noted his awareness of this when he wrote (in the original score) the words 'NB this piece always has B natural instead of B flat'. It is often said that his adherence to the mode is more rigorous than would have been possible in the sixteenth century, but the examples of Lydian tonality given by Glareanus are no less free from *musica ficta.*

I have already mentioned Josquin (see p. 14) and it is a miracle of art for Beethoven to attain, in his visionary hymn, the inexplicable perfection and simplicity of a composer whose work was the culmination of a universal style already established by Dunstable and transmitted by such great masters as Dufay and Ockeghem.

Each of the five phrases is harmonised in the purest ancient style. The F mode allowing no dominant seventh (B for B flat), Beethoven's note-against-note writing suggests a shadowy C major when F and B natural are sounded together in what to nineteenth-century ears is the dominant seventh of that key. The use of such chords is not a breach of medieval tradition; the style known as 'English descant' allowed and, for all we know, rejoiced in the rich sound of such progressions as these:

Ex. 15

In 'te Domine
(late 13th cent.)

The D major *Andante* that, with total discontinuity, follows the
close of the hymn is described by Beethoven as 'Neue Kraft fühlend'
('feeling renewed strength'), but the original gloss spoke of a renewal of strength and feeling (sensibility). The experience represented in the hymn is not received through the senses; hence the
change of superscription.

The *Andante,* with its trills and grace-notes, breaks forth into joy
with the innocence of George Herbert.

> And now in age I bud again,
> After so many deaths I live and write;
> I once more smell the dew and rain,
> And relish versing: O my only light,
> > It cannot be
> > That I am he
> On whom thy tempests fell all night.

The return to the *Molto adagio* of the 'Heiliger Dankgesang' is
mediated by the calmer melody (significantly marked both *cantabile*
and *espressivo*) at bar 67. The hymn now floats serenely above suspensions not heard – but for some passing wonders in the finale of
Mozart's 'Jupiter' symphony–since Bach's 'Dorian' fugue. The contrast between Lydian F and D is now established, and the return to
the *Andante* is given tonal solidity by a dominant seventh on the
last beat (cf. bars 30 and 114). The movement's formal scheme (A-B-
A-B-A) needs this return, but whereas the hymn, in its affinity with
the old chorale partitas, virtually demands variation, the contrasting
section is already on its first appearance a variation on an unstated
theme, and further elaboration would be unsatisfactory. By attend-
ing to his unspecific programme Beethoven solves also the formal
problem. Clearly the contrast between the deepest utterance of
'Gratias ago tibi' and the glow of returning strength is not to be
elaborated once stated, and the second version of the *Andante* makes
definite figures (for example, scales) out of the fragmented decorations of the first statement. What was a hope is now actual. Observe
how the hesitant bass of bars 55 ff. on its second reappearance turns

into the sturdy pizzicato of bar 141ff. As before, at the end the 6/3 chord of C major quietly dismisses modern tonality; what remains is either the most authentic spiritual illumination in music, or the incomprehensible abstract of a genius out of touch with reality. In this final section everything is at first dissolved in the third version of the preludial phrase to which Beethoven now accords his rarely-used 'mit innigster Empfindung' ('with the most inward feeling or perception'). This means neither *espressivo* nor *cantabile*; it is written over the first movement of Op. 101 and the variation theme of Op. 109, but is used nowhere else in the quartets. The entry of the hymn is hidden, both by the tying of its first unison note to the previous quaver and by the unprepared G' in the viola (bar 170). Even this first of the five lines in psalm metre is represented only by five of its eight minims treated in imitative counterpoint; the full phrase is delayed until bar 184. The polyphony here has been called medieval, but the description is neither accurate nor adequate to the remoteness of this music from all historical styles. Beethoven intuitively rediscovers the severe diatonic dissonances of thirteenth-century Ars Antiqua, combined with a non-harmonic counterpoint in which parts cross like tenor and contra-tenor in the early fifteenth century, as though the concept of the triad and its inversions belonged to a future age.

If this hyperbole seems unwarranted, consider one or two instances. First the treatment of the hymn phrase in bars 170ff. Even without the brief suspensions of the prelude phrase, this passage belongs to a pre-Renaissance world into which an emancipated dominant seventh has insinuated itself. Later, after the mysterious cadence in D minor (bars 181–2) where the C sharps and open fifth (A-E) transport the hearer for a moment into the late fifteenth century, the parts move in a heterophony utterly at variance with all classical styles—Ex. 16 overleaf.

The climax to which all this moves is Cistercian in its grandeur, rejecting with such severity all that could give pleasure that Palestrina by contrast sounds positively worldly in his beautifully-spaced euphony of choral voices. Here too the plainest diatonic progressions are transformed into something never heard before; the F major tonic chord of the modal key is not merely in 6/4 position, but of its seven notes five are given to the bass, and the notoriously rich-sounding dominant ninth is hardly recognisable on the second minim of bar 192. Awe and dread have taken the place of the con-

Ex. 16
bars185 ff.
Vlns. I/II

templative ecstasy of the *Adagio* in Op. 59 no. 2.

From the beginning, the strict Lydian harmony has barely sustained an F tonic against the pressure of C major, and the diminuendo after the climax seems to be concerned with a coda in this over-weighty dominant. The final stroke of harmonic imagination is to reinvent the interrupted cadence (better designated by the German *Trugschluss* – 'deceptive close') so that the 'wrong' chord shows itself as the right one with irresistibly calm certainty. Finally, even the preludial phrase ('mit innigster Empfindung') dissolves into the first two notes of the hymn.

Op. 132 was originally intended to be in four movements, and at one early stage Beethoven sketched, as second movement according to Nottebohm, a 'marcia serioso pathet [?]'. This description does not fit the ironically cheerful *Alla marcia, assai vivace* that follows the Lydian end of the *Adagio,* but both are related to the march in the sonata Op. 101. Here is the discarded sketch:

Ex. 17
marcia serioso pathet [?]

As far back as Op. 10 no. 3, Beethoven had encountered the problem of finding a sequel to a slow movement of exceptional gravity, and his solutions are as various as the pieces they follow. In the early piano sonata the tragic intensity of the *Largo e mesto* precludes any drastic contrast, and the exquisitely pensive *Menuetto* is admirably free from Romantic 'consolation' – a type of contrast supplied with fatal ease by some later composers. A similar decorum may be seen in Op. 59 no. 2.

In Op. 132 discontinuity of style and mood is unmistakable, and the A major march needs none of the distortion and parodistic irony of the corresponding movement in Op. 101. In fact, out of context, the piece would be thoroughly agreeable (no ambiguity should be looked for in the *dolce* marked at the double bar). Here, though, the context gives the meaning, and the harmlessly mundane interlude takes on an appalling banality (it is not really at all commonplace; note the fine thematic imitations in the *dolce* section), and its innocent demolition of the sublime *Adagio* can lead only to disaster. (Its first figure may be seen as a parody of the rising major sixth that begins the 'Heiliger Dankgesang'.) Where we expect the trio section to begin, a mournful phrase from the first movement materialises (see also Op. 127 third movement, bars 70ff.):

Ex. 18
bars 25-26
Op. 132, IV
Più allegro

bars 188-9
Op. 132, I

Astonishingly, it introduces a quotation of the second instrumental recitative in the Ninth Symphony (finale, bars 56ff.), cheapened by a tremolando accompaniment which itself debases the quartet medium. The pathetic appoggiatura of operatic recitative becomes increasingly prominent, and the mood of savage mockery or feigned tragedy is unmistakable when the first violin's frantic cadenza emerges from a shrill diminished seventh.

The noble sombre theme of the finale was, as is well known, first sketched for the Ninth Symphony, and its presence here is further evidence of the fragmented construction of this quartet, with its extensive quotations from earlier compositions in the second movement. The gradual emergence of the perfected melody from diverse sketches may be traced in a few quotations. The earliest source is the D minor theme headed 'Finale instromentale', written before June 1823 (Ex. 19a). A later revision, still for the symphony, contains a figure reminiscent of the first movement of Op. 59 no. 2(b). Later in 1823 Beethoven returned to the theme, which acquired a new figure (c). The idea was altogether abandoned when he decided on the chorale finale for the symphony, and when a year later he began work on the finale of Op. 132 he noted a quite different theme (d), followed by a variant of the Ninth Symphony idea, beginning with another and much closer reminiscence of Op. 59 no. 2 (e).

Ex. 19(a)

Finale instromentale

(b)
bars 6 ff.
Op. 132, IV, sketch

bars 13 ff.
Op. 59, No. 2, I

The great melody on which Beethoven builds the finest and last of all his tragic (or pathetic) rondos sounds like a spontaneous invention, but to compare it with the above quotations shows how astonishingly it was assembled from them:

The instrumental texture is as masterly as it is original; without simulating orchestral effects, Beethoven produces a depth and amplitude of symphonic grandeur. Note the double-stops of the viola on the second beat. The second return of the rondo is another triumph of the deaf composer's instrumental imagination. When it begins in D minor the insistent falling semitone of the accompaniment rises to the surface, with intensely quiet pathos, in the colour of the cello's A string, over the grave C string tone of the viola (see bars 164ff.). When the main episode is recapitulated we recognise its affinity with the 'motto' theme of the first movement. It also resembles, though in less drastic contrast with its surroundings, the *una corda* section in the finale of the 'Hammerklavier' sonata.

This expansion of the eight-bar episode early in the movement gives the whole passage a quiet breadth that makes the accelerando distressing as well as unexpected. For nine bars before the *Presto* the violin insists, with an intensity on the verge of hysteria, on the reiterated F-E cell from the first bars of the movement. This, followed by the cello's delivery of the rondo theme in its highest possible register, produces scarcely endurable tension, belonging to the world of twentieth-century Expressionism and unparalleled in Beethoven. Nor does the turn to the tonic major presage a happy conclusion. The Ländler rhythm from the second movement returns near the end (*col punto d'arco*) with hallucinatory effect; there is barely time for the recovery of the rational will in the closing unison.

No other composition in all Beethoven's works shows the unintegrated contrasts of this quartet, but once he had become possessed by the unique vision of the 'Heiliger Dankgesang', no solution of the formal problem was available other than to surround it with sound-images united only by their total diversity. The only common factor, itself made obligatory by the diatonic severity of the Lydian sections, is an extraordinarily narrow range of tonality, far more restricted than would be possible in mature Haydn or Mozart, though familiar enough in the Baroque concerto.

Only the outer movements show the unity of the other late quartets, and the familiar critical approach that seeks to group the three middle works in some imagined relatedness not shared by Op. 127 and Op. 135 misses the mark sadly, misled as it is by the *ignis fatuus* of related themes.

Op. 130 in B flat major

From a letter Beethoven wrote to his nephew in August 1825 it appears that Op. 132 was to have had six movements, presumably including the *Alla tedesca* in A major as well as the present second movement. By November Op. 130 was finished, and Beethoven told Holz that a new idea that had come to him would have to be reserved for the next quartet but one (Op. 131), as the latest (Op. 130) already had too many movements. The sense of tension, of dissociation in Op. 132, with its diverse styles and unrelated themes, vanishes with Op. 130 and Op. 131, even greater works that can afford to revive the formal pattern of the old divertimento, used by Beethoven for his first successful work for strings, the fine Trio in E flat, Op. 3. In its original form, with the final fugue, Op. 130 has inspired much speculative writing and industrious analysis; the existence of such commentaries is a kind of tribute to the greatness of the work, but at the same time suggests that special gifts are necessary to the hearer who hopes to understand it. Beethoven himself did not set out to write the 'music of the future', and the last quartets were in fact played and admired in spite of their formidable technical difficulty. Op. 130 was first heard in Vienna on 21 March 1826, and even the fugue was not unanimously rejected; his surprising readiness to substitute a less forbidding movement shows his concern with promoting performances of his new works. It was the long neglect of the Romantic era, not the indifference of his contemporaries, that produced the myth of the misunderstood genius withdrawing from a world with which he could no longer communicate. The human, as distinct from the musical, wonder of the last quartets lies in Beethoven's untroubled concentration on the perfecting of these compositions at a time when his life was full of disaster. One is reminded of Mozart; Beethoven rediscovers, after the mighty rhetoric and communal eloquence of his middle years, the Mozartian lightness of touch.

The slow introduction to the first movement brings back the serene objectivity of Op. 127, after the brooding intensity of Op. 132. Formal cadences are the first topic, with a chromatic inflection carried over into the quaver dialogue begun by the cello in the seventh bar. The chromaticism, be it noted, is not pathetic or yearning, but as purely musical as Bach's in, for instance, the C sharp major fugue ('48', Book II), or indeed the fugue that follows the *Chromatic Fantasia* – a work well known to Beethoven.

The two ideas that constitute the first theme of the *Allegro* seem to be designed for the greatest possible contrast with the *Adagio* – a running pattern of Bach-like objectivity (fig. a) and a rising fourth (fig. b) harmonised in the plainest tonic-dominant alternation. Besides its obvious connection with the fugue of the 'Hammerklavier' sonata, the semiquaver figure occurs in the D major cello sonata.

Ex. 21

There is nothing very individual in this idea, but oddly enough the fourths may be recognised in the other sonata of Op. 102. Both are formulas, but so are many themes in some of Mozart's ripest works (consider the quintets K.515 and 614: K.516 is far closer to Op. 132), and the emotional neutrality of this opening makes possible its premature interruption by the *Adagio,* with its grave melody concealed in the two lowest voices. Just how far Beethoven proposes to go in the direction of classical formula is apparent in the bass of bars 34–7, a tag far older than Handel or Bach.

Ex. 22

Parody would be too strong a term for this good-humoured play with obsolete modes of speech, evident too in the transition to the flat submediant for the second subject, a transition effected by a deliberately spelled out chromatic scale. The new theme (bars 55 ff.) with its rising minor sixth (complete with portamento) has an operatic *espressivo,* as of a character who can regard himself with self-deprecating irony. No good sonata movement can live entirely on contrasts (or on total thematic unity for that matter), and the ingratiating melody derives from the introduction:

With admirable subtlety Beethoven relates the first subject to the *Adagio,* indirectly, by associating with the G flat melody the four semiquavers of its opening phrase. The veiled tone colour of strings in this flat key is enhanced by the cello's *sotto voce,* beginning high on the fourth string. Everything is remote and mysteriously quiet, as though we overhear a conversation full of meaning that somehow eludes us, though its complete lucidity is not to be mistaken. The preparation for the second subject has been staunchly orthodox in its approach to the home dominant, and the elusiveness of Beethoven's humour becomes plain when the unexpected G flat is made insecure by the lack of emphasis on its own dominant. So, when the repeat of the exposition abruptly reinstates the tonic, the absence of surprise is itself surprising. The recapitulation will show all this in a different light. The repeat (to omit it betrays gross insensitivity) gives emphasis to the *Adagio* (which never recurs complete) and so, by association, to the light-hearted self-mockery of the pensive figure from bars 10 and 12 (see bars 37–40). Perhaps, too, a second hearing confirms the faith of those who find in the closing octaves a reflection of the first phrase of the movement—Ex. 24 overleaf. It has been claimed that Beethoven took such derivations and far more recondite ones for granted; if so he must have regarded them as too obvious to require thought, as no trace of such processes appears in his sketches.

Returning to matters of more aesthetic significance, let us note how the persistent cadential figure that runs through the develop-

Ex. 24

ment (it similarly pervades Schubert's song *Geheimes*, composed in
1821) is carefully prepared, together with the two phrases from the
first subject. It depends for its strange beauty on the transference to
the bass of the rising cadence heard in the fourth bar of the introduction, and this happens, for the first time, in bar 99. When the
cello hands over to the viola the reiteration of the two notes required
to maintain the pattern, and sings in its most winning tenor a fragment of a tune derived from the G flat 'second subject', the syn-
thesis is complete.

Ex. 25

This brief development brings together, with relaxed casualness as
it appears, the essentials of all the main themes.

In this dance of blessed spirits the cadence figure murmurs as
tirelessly as the brook in the 'Pastoral' symphony, while cello and
violin pursue a dialogue of blissful levity. At first the violin answers
the cello's mock-ardent declaration with the upward fourth of the
first subject, but having heard the rising octave for the third time
imitates it in the rhythm of its own theme. 'You have forgotten
your lines', says the cello, and prompts his colleague twice with the
fourth D-G. By way of riposte the violin takes over the cello tune as
G major drifts into C minor. In three attempts the cello has been
unable to complete the phrase, but at its fourth appearance a con-

flation of the two ideas makes a rounded statement, with the disputed fourth parodied as a major third!

Ex. 26

bars 125 ff.

C major, thus introduced by sleight, is not to be accepted, for the recapitulation is about to break in. So E flat is restored and it is, after all, the violin that brings back the main tonic and the first subject by diverting the second bar of the cello melody.

The first subject, now far too confident to yield to the *Adagio* as in the exposition, is tonally secure enough to vary its sturdily diatonic motto with the wonderful augmented-triad harmony in bar 140 and the diminished seventh two bars later, both motivated by the cello. The *Adagio* seems to have retreated beyond reach, so there is no point in repeating the mocking of its most expressive phrase (compare the single bar 147 with the four bars 37–40 in the exposition). As for the transition, it would be banal to recapitulate the emphatic preparation of a key not to be stated, and, instead of the original dominant preparation, Beethoven makes a series of modulations that move steadily towards D flat, where the viola reintroduces the second subject melody, now adorned with chromatic inflections that give it a Gioconda smile to which a naïve response would be inadvisable. Having arrived at the dominant of B flat, it is more decorously recapitulated in the home tonic, followed by the remainder of the expository material until those impressive octaves arouse expectation of a return of the *Adagio*. This time the two tempi are set in direct confrontation, so that proximity enforces reconciliation. The brief coda, all conflict ended, begins with a marvellously rich harmonisation of the chromatic cadence figure from bars 3 and 4 and ends happily with a final reference to the 'motto' fourth, now overlapping in treble and bass, to make four bars representing the broad tonic and dominant swing of the middle-period codas.

To find even a remote model for the *Presto* we must look back to the F minor *Allegretto* of the piano sonata Op. 10 no. 2 (I attach no significance to the fact that the finale of the sonata uses the semiquaver-quaver figure in the first movement of Op. 130), which has the same quiet strength with, however, an undertone of pathos that could not survive for a moment the unemphatic impact of the later piece. It would seem reasonable to expect, after the un-tragic first movement, a Beethoven scherzo in triple time, and in the major key. This expectation is partly met, but the scherzo appears as trio section to the *Presto,* in a new kind of A-B-A form. Beethoven's friends knew he was happy when he indulged in puns from which the Marx Brothers might flinch, and the chromatic slides, longer each time, which lead back to the reprise bring the same kind of humour into a work otherwise notably aloof and unresponsive to an over-familiar approach. The reprise, by varying its repeats as in double variations, produces some very odd part-writing between second violin and viola that could be called eccentric but for its delightful euphony. Theories of music as emotional language or as the externalisation of the artist's aggression are calmly rebuked by the untroubled perfection of this *jeu d'esprit.*

So far Op. 130 has failed to provide a message to humanity, at any rate of the kind to be expected by seekers after Matthew Arnold's 'morality tinged with emotion'. Beethoven's slow movements after the Second Symphony had maintained, in all their depth and variety, a high seriousness whether elegiac, contemplative or lyrical. One exception comes to mind, the *Adagio grazioso* of the sonata Op. 31 no. 1, a piece indubitably beautiful but showing a dangerous tendency to make fun of its own exquisite sensibility. The first slow movement of Op. 130 is a divertimento, of which the tone is set by the two introductory bars (marked *Preludio* in a sketch) where a chromatic step (possibly derived from the first-movement *Adagio*) over expressive harmonies bears the marking *poco scherzando*. As so often in this quartet, the theme itself is given in the dark colour of the viola's low register, to be repeated in full by the first violin, both over a far from serious staccato bass, as in the second variation of Op. 127. The key is D flat (G in an early sketch), but not for long: by the fifth bar the harmony is brightening, with G naturals, and the pizzicato full close in the dominant brings a new theme. It seems rather Beckmesser-like to call this a sonata exposition, especially as the first theme reappears in or around F major with delightfully casual hints at polyphony until it yields place to a third melody (significantly marked *cantabile* and *dolce*) in the reinstated dominant. The accompaniment, of fantastic delicacy, transforms the classical

quartet into an instrument unknown to the sublunar world, a marvellous instance of the deaf master's endless inventiveness and
scientific precision in the imagining of unheard sonorities.

With the mysterious lucidity characteristic of this quartet, the
new theme expands and develops, merged with the 'second subject',
then with the introductory bars, which also have the rhythmic figure

♩ ♩. ♫. This being also a feature of the first theme, a return
is easily effected, and what follows may be accurately designated
'recapitulation'. Sonata however is a style, not a form, and depends
on contrasts organised around the main structural features. Beethoven is not concerned in this *Andante* with action of a kind that
can exploit the tensions of opposed tonalities or of rhythmic development: it begins at the point where conflicts have been resolved
and is too animated for contemplation, too calm for drama. Certainly the first theme returns in the tonic, after the introductory
'sigh' has appeared in the bass, but the pervasive element of bene-
volent wilfulness so evident in this work causes the theme to lose
its way, and the sequential bar has to be repeated. By now we recognise the habit of failing to complete a statement which it shares
with the cello melody in the first movement's development. The
other themes return with varied tonality until we arrive at a pause
on the tonic, disguised as the dominant of the subdominant, in
which the previous bars have settled. After the violin has run up a
long scale (the extension of the detail introduced in the 'development') there is a leisurely and unambiguous close in G flat. Beethoven now seems to recollect that his expressive falling semitone
(the 'sigh') is related to a wonderful passage in the slow movement
of the 'Jupiter' symphony, but whereas Mozart's chromatic harmony
is made out of 'dominant' sevenths in root position, Beethoven
places beneath his sequence of broken tritones more Bach-like progressions with diminished chords, the one on the fourth beat being
dwelt on for a whole bar until all sense of the main tonic is, for the
moment, lost in the reverberation of this ambiguous harmony. (It
was not for nothing that he had copied out the recitative sections of
Bach's *Chromatic Fantasia*.) It resolves, incredibly, on to a chord of
A major; restated with enharmonic spelling (D♭ for C♯), the diminished seventh is softened until the 'sigh' (its meanings are subtle
beyond verbalisation, like Weelkes's 'Fa la' in 'O care') dissolves in
a marvellous sequence unmistakably related to the Mozart theme.

The rest of the coda consists almost of quotations from various themes in a quite unclassical assemblage of fragments, the strangest of all being the momentary diverting of a cadence from the tonic into B flat, the main key of the quartet.

When Beethoven took up again the *Alla tedesca* he had sketched in A major for Op. 132 he wrote it first in B flat, with a too-sophisticated chromatic step soon to be excised:

Ex. 27

Allemande-Allegro

Remembering that the *Grosse Fuge* was planned as finale, we note that by choosing G major for his second scherzo Beethoven placed in the centre of the quartet a movement making a tonal division like some geological fault in a range of hills. G major has been heard in a B flat context during the first movement, but its recurrence after D flat creates the maximum discontinuity, reinforced by a section in the subdominant of this very unrelated key. The piece itself, in its unequivocal innocence, remains unaccountable to analysis, whether tonal, thematic or rhythmic. On the surface, contrast is absolute; at a level deeper than reasoning the sequence of movements in this enigmatic quartet bears the mark of truth.

The Cavatina, like the B flat theme in the slow movement of the Ninth Symphony, represents a kind of personal utterance far more uncommon in Beethoven's music than would be recognised by upholders of the immature notion that the artist's aim is self-expression. Reliable anecdotes attest to the deep emotional significance of this *Adagio* to its composer, who for once was impelled to lower the defences against the world of which he had felt the necessity as far back as the 'Heiligenstadt Testament'. The *Arioso dolente* of Op. 110 has the same directness of utterance, and it is notable that both pieces bear designations associated with opera – Arioso and Cavatina. Even the C flat section marked *beklemmt* (= 'beklommen' *sc.* 'oppressed') speaks with the accents of King Lear; the greatest masters do not yearn, and the whole of this most moving of *Adagio*s is characterised by a noble restraint looking back to the world of Bach rather than forward to the emotional excesses of self-enjoying Romantic sorrow. Beethoven's griefs were real and devastating and are not fit subject for public discussion.

In the tonal scheme of Op. 130 the *Danza alla tedesca* could have led directly to the finale (i.e. the Fugue), but in a work where, as the listener gradually realises, extreme contrasts in every element of composition are to be resolved in a finale of unprecedented size (the most drastic solution of the 'finale problem' implicit in the classical sonata) a deeply-felt slow movement is necessary if the resolution of conflicts is to be adequately motivated. This, incidentally, is the case against performing the *Grosse Fuge* as a separate work – it arises out of nothing, and the second finale does not so much re-place it as provide an alternative solution to the unintegrated se-quence of the earlier movements. There are no 'inevitable' solutions of the problems of order and sequence in even the greatest compos-itions. To praise a work for its inevitability is to express enthusiasm for its combination of beauty and power, but the composer's free will is never compromised and he is bound only by his own discrim-ination. Op. 130 must be considered as a work planned to end with a vast fugue, but the existence of the second finale is proof that Beethoven regarded a different conclusion as aesthetically valid: the listener's awareness of the difference is of course retrospective, an obvious point sometimes overlooked by commentators who treat musical structures as though they were solid objects.

Beethoven's knowledge of fugue was not only based on the greatest of models, but lay in the depths of his own musical experi-ence. When as a boy he learned the '48' with Neefe, he must have recognised that he was being introduced to the deepest mysteries of the art he was to practise, and his later studies with Albrechts-berger were to gain facility in a style, not to acquire the knowledge he already possessed.

When Mozart discovered Bach his own genius was approaching maturity, and the effect was disturbing rather than inspiring, as may be seen from the Köchel numbers that identify not finished com-positions but fugues that failed to get beyond their expositions. This is the only section of a fugue for which Bach could provide a model, for the sufficient reason that all his fugues are different – fugue being, as Tovey pointed out, a texture, not a form.

The problem for the Viennese masters was to absorb into the sonata style a kind of music which rarely permitted the element of recapitulation: even Bach's few examples of *da capo* type fugues may not have been known to Beethoven. In so far as generalisation is possible with Bach, it can be said that whereas the exposition of a fugue will establish the subject of discourse in a way not totally unlike that of sonata, the sequel will not initiate tonal action, i.e. the tonic will be always within reach, so that no dramatic return to it will be possible. Even stretto, prescribed by academic theory as a means of producing a final climax, is sometimes used by Bach to make a concentration of textural density in the middle of a fugue. The B flat minor fugue ('48', Bk. II) displays stretti considerably more grand than the final two-part combination by inversion doubled in thirds, which can scarcely be felt as a high point of polyphonic argument.

For Beethoven then the problem lay not in exposition, but in the disposition of tonal and rhythmic contrasts. In Op. 106, where, as in the quartet, the use of fugue as a finale raised the further problem of the all-sufficing coda, he adopted one of Bach's solutions, following perhaps the famous A minor organ fugue, but this expansion into instrumental rhetoric natural to the keyboard was inadmissible in a quartet. The irrelevance of all these classical precedents enforced the total originality of the *Grosse Fuge*. It has been exhaustively analysed, but the elucidation of its structural basis contributes little to the understanding of this strange composition. Indeed, by revealing a solid and seemingly comprehensible formal scheme, analysis may impede understanding at the deeper level by obscuring the essential relationship of the fugue to the preceding movements of the quartet to which it belongs. To separate it from these antecedents is rather like presenting the last act of a Shakespeare play without the rest. From the 'Eroica' onwards Beethoven's major works (apart from concertos, where a quite different pattern prevails) resolved in a finale the tensions and contrasts of earlier movements: in Op. 130 the contrasts are so extreme, alike in key, texture and rhythm, that only a finale of quite extraordinary range could hope to reconcile them and give a conclusive unity to the whole work.

The oddly-named Overtura is itself a paradigm of contrast in unity, setting out several versions of the theme, with its reference back to the beginning of the quartet—Ex. 28 opposite. In this prologue, it prefigures the action to follow but not, be it noted, in the 'right' order. First comes the form used in the A flat fugue and later in the coda, next the combination with the semiquaver figure of the G flat episode, and only then the enigmatic rhythmic shape of the first fugue. The repeated tied notes off the beat are

Ex. 28(a)

anticipated in the Cavatina and earlier, of course, in Op. 110.

The two themes of this double fugue embody the enforced association of extreme contrasts that characterises Op. 130. Whereas the 'motto' belongs to the Bach world, as may be seen if we 'normalise' its rhythmic pattern,

Ex. 29

its companion is aggressively 'ordinary' both in its sequential pattern and its obsessively unvaried metre. Extensive sketching was needed before Beethoven arrived at this very unclassical combination, but the fugue, once launched, acquires from the interaction of macro- and micro-rhythms a controlled violence without parallel in music before the twentieth century and anticipated only by Mozart in the grim C minor fugue for two pianos (K.426), where linear writing is in fact even more uncompromising. Evidently Mozart's fugue impressed Beethoven, for he copied it out in score. The unrelenting fortissimo of this first fugue arises from its structure; Beethoven played the organ and must have recognised the inappropriateness of dynamic changes in many a Bach fugue, though it is only in early compositions, e.g. the F minor fugue, BWV 534, that Bach shows such a restricted tonal scheme. Again we recognise how the whole plan of the *Grosse Fuge*

45

is related to the rest of Op. 130, where the tonic major has scarcely been present after the first movement. The B flat fugue develops neither harmonically nor in theme but in rhythm. Although triplet figures appear as early as bar 58, the dotted rhythm persists unbroken until bar 139, where both subjects are compressed into a form in which it is not present, its absence bringing the only relief of tension since the beginning of the piece. The combination of the triplet version of the second theme with the one-quaver displacement of the main subject produces a rhythmic complexity unparalleled since the late fourteenth century.

Tempering its aggressive fury, the fugue gains in power, but before it can subside the dotted rhythm reappears and almost prevails as the tonality begins to shift away from B flat (bars 153-8). When the episode prefigured in the Overtura begins in G flat memory relates both contrasts, of texture and key, to the fantasy-world of the first movement. Beethoven's master-stroke here is to make the most extreme contrast in this work by transforming the ideas of the terrifying B flat fugue into a discourse of extreme euphony. The motto of the finale, first diminished, then in longer notes, combines with a gently murmuring sequential melody that clearly derives from the upper component of the double fugue. To complete the reconciliation of opposites Beethoven exchanges their rhythmic characters: the accents of the motto, transferred to the upper theme, become a gentle displacement over the barline, and the motto itself now moves in a long phrase of even crotchets. Throughout this interlude polyphony is dissolved into a texture where fugue-like entries can appear freed of all argumentative logic. Even the extension of the theme, in close imitation between treble and bass in bars 193ff., is completely unrhetorical, and it vanishes before the one dynamic change, the crescendo to f in bar 220. The unison that follows is broken by the cello's insistence on the figure that had appeared in the first fugue after the close in D minor at bar 109—Ex. 30 opposite.

This reminiscence is surely designed to begin the destruction of the visionary calm that has prevailed since the end of the B flat fugue. As the semiquavers descend, the octaves of violins and viola that have already evoked a recollection of the end of the exposition in the first movement of the quartet become an unmistakable allusion. In the 'Appassionata' the more primitive intermezzo makes a calm between two storms with an almost Romantic directness of emo-

Ex. 30(a)

(b)

tional appeal no longer valid for the Beethoven of 1825; the G flat episode makes a response too deep to permit a return to the first fugue. Had Beethoven intended this he would have written something less compellingly truthful in its beauty, but the possibility of taking the 6/8 version of the motto as the beginning of the end is also excluded by the sheer magnitude of the opening fugue, of which the violent force can neither be resumed nor dismissed by a 'triumphant' coda. Refusing to anticipate, the listener knows at this stage in the work only that the theme, its aggression purged away, has become the subject of a very unfugal discourse with the abrupt shake from the Overtura (bar 10) explained away as a cadential trill and the upper theme of the B flat fugue made into the most accommodating of conventional basses.

As in the Agnus Dei of the *Missa Solemnis,* confidence thus easily gained is illusory: the cheerful cadence in B flat is contemptuously pushed aside by the most contradictory of keys, its own flat seventh, and the second fugue begins in A flat. The subject reproduces exactly its rhythmic shape as heard in the first bars of the Overtura with (a significant detail) the final trill prolonged. The counter-sub-

47

ject, a double-diminution of a fragment of the theme, has already appeared in the G flat interlude. It is dangerously easy to trace connections that have no function because they are not presented with a view to audibility, but this figure is 'placed' in the only unharmonised passage of the whole G flat section.

Ex. 31

With the answer (viola, bar 280) a further counter-subject is added, also based on the theme, but this is a kind of fugue where no theme is long preserved unaltered, whereas the B flat fugue, for all its violence and 'linear' harshness, had retained classical procedures (this is true also of the fugues in Op. 106, the *Missa Solemnis* and Op. 131). Beethoven now creates a new art form – fugue-cum-variation. By sheer intuition, he rediscovers the Ars Nova technique of isorhythm. If the metrical shape of a theme is maintained, the notes may be altered – the rhythm is the theme. In sonata and rondo this idea had been used by Beethoven, but here he adds it to the resources of fugue. The second countersubject (this is still the exposition!) may best be described thus 𝅗𝅥. | 𝅗𝅥. 𝅗𝅥 𝄾 | three times plus a concluding figure. Melodically it derives, of course, from the first three notes of the main subject, but its identity depends on rhythm and the rhetoric is cumulative to the magnificent bass sequence in bars 299ff. Meanwhile the main subject is extended by sequential treatment of its cadential trill (bars 305–9) and this, in thirds, becomes the material of an episode, modulating grandly in antiphony, first between middle and outer voices, then (bars 340ff.) in three parts together, as in Mozart's writing for quintet. Up to this point everything in the *Grosse Fuge* has been driven along a narrow tonal road, and the sense of release is unmistakable now as the two-bar phrases multiply. If the main theme can expand, it can also contract. In the episode it is represented by its last bars, i.e. the portion after the long notes; now the beginning plus the end may stand for the whole subject.

Ex. 32
bar 349

The quotation shows the wildly jubilant counter-melody, forged out of the first three notes of the main subject, which accompanies the entries of its condensed version. When the first violin states the full subject for the first time since the exposition, its closing trill persists over a canonic dialogue between viola and cello where the theme has its most characteristic interval represented by a crush-note. In this section of the fugue, Beethoven writes in a style that cannot be called prophetic, as no one has had either the boldness or the creative energy to imitate him here. Artists are praised by historians for their anticipation of later techniques, an element interesting only to connoisseurs of precedence, and meaningless with the passage of time. How shall we praise Beethoven then for inventing a music beyond the historical process? The just word is Stravinsky's – no idle hyperbole but a precise statement of the truth: 'This absolutely contemporary piece of music that will be contemporary for ever.' The power of this climax comes from its underlying harmonic structure, which is of Bach-like symmetry. Any expressionist can produce an effect of chaotic violence, but Beethoven never lost touch with the Age of Reason. There is a background of perfectly normal harmonic progressions supporting the ceaseless trills of the first violin, the weird figure of the counter-theme in the second, and the relentless canon of the two lower parts. Notice how the treble line conceals beneath its trill the descending figure of the theme first heard at the very beginning of the piece. Its emergence at the change of key to E flat, in combination with the most extreme variant of the motto theme, has a dramatic impact not excelled by anything in the sonata style, to which drama is a natural resource. It is a notable triumph of mind to achieve this in the first and only example of fugue-variation-sonata (Liszt's B minor sonata can manage only the most perfunctory of quasi-fugal gestures). Tonally the *Grosse Fuge* remains up to this point strange, though too magisterially impressive to be called obscure. E flat, which might seem to be a step towards the long-absent B flat tonic, is only the dominant of A flat, to which anomalous centre the music returns for the powerful restatement of the G flat intermezzo; powerful instead of lyrical, in accordance with the principle of contrast that runs through the whole finale. Every theme appears in two broadly antithetical forms, and before the coda can bring back the transfigured double subject of the B flat fugue, we must be confronted with the reverse process applied to the ethereal intermezzo.

The return to the *Allegro molto* is effected in a passage of a rhythmic subtlety surely intended to obliterate all sense of movement; thus the re-establishment of B flat as main tonic (at last!) is deprived of any sonata-type impact. No sonata movement could possibly reserve its return to the tonic for its coda, and the very obvious element of recapitulation here is of a transition, not of anything that could be regarded as expository. What we expect, from knowledge of Beethoven's earlier music, is a triumphant coda, a type of conclusion in which he had displayed mastery over thirty years, thus setting a precedent – he is not to be blamed for its consequences. Beethoven's triumphs ring true, because they represent the response to experience of an artist to whom heroic resolution came naturally, all the more convincing through the background awareness of mutability. With the F minor quartet the finale problem demanded a different way of ending a large sonata design; opinion remains divided over the degree of Beethoven's success here. In Op. 127 a sturdily 'normal' last movement can move, in its coda, from the etherealisation of its Haydnesque theme to an 'Eroica'-like apotheosis. Here the coda makes an expansion of the meanings latent in the theme.

With Op. 130, though, the finale becomes almost a fugal half of a vast fantasia and fugue, where the fantasia is a sequence of contrasts scarcely comprehensible as a unity unless in retrospect. Besides resolving the conflicts of the fugue, the coda must at least evoke the beginning of the whole quartet, though thematic links of the kind so laboriously manufactured by commentators would be an otiose resource that Beethoven would scorn to use. First, then, the scherzo-like interlude heard before the A flat fugue returns in a surprisingly literal repetition. At the point where in its first appearance it had been crushed by the A flat tonality, it now continues in a leisurely expansion of the inflected semitones of the motto theme in harmonies as sensuously appealing as Mozart's in many such passages. Without any direct reference, these warm chromatic touches are reminiscent of the quite untragic seriousness of the quartet's opening bars. Compare the semitone figures in this coda (bars 565ff.) with Ex. 29 and with the theme in bars 7-13 of the first movement. All this connects with the opening of the third movement and, perhaps, with the alternately falling and rising semitones in the main tune of the *Alla danza tedesca*.

Be that as it may, what is unmistakable is the heavenly levity of the now transfigured themes from the fugue itself, with felicities of tone-colour lost, it would seem, on those who maintain that Beethoven was indifferent to the quartet medium in these last works. Note the crossing of cello and viola in bars 573-80 and the delectable pizzicato in bars 596-608. Beethoven, who could thus translate the awe-inspiring *terribiltà* of his fugue subjects, would surely have appreciated Jowett's apocryphal query in the Beerbohm cartoon: 'And what were they going to do with the Grail when they'd found it, Mr Rossetti?' Before the still not-imminent end, not merely of the *Grosse Fuge* but of the largest string quartet ever written, the opening of the Overtura is recapitulated in the tonic, a necessary structural device. (Note that the tempo is quicker than at the beginning.) It is preceded by the thematic quotations that originally followed it, and in reverse order. The grim B flat fugue combination is now broken off abruptly at the point where it suggests subdominant harmony, as does the whispered hint of the G flat intermezzo. This dissolving of all tensions is a deeply mysterious process and has nothing of mundane ease or comfort in its calm intellectual triumph. The final word is the statement, as grand as anything in the *Art of Fugue,* of the double-theme combination from the beginning of the B flat fugue, in bars 707-16 (note the depth of tone in the octave doubling of the lower theme).

At the first performance of the complete quartet Beethoven showed no pleasure at the applause evoked by the two scherzo movements, but was indignant at the audience's failure to appreciate the fugue. (An anonymous critic wrote in 1826: '. . . as incomprehensible as Chinese. Monstrous difficulties . . . music to please the inhabitants of Morocco'.) Nonetheless, he consented to separate publication of the fugue, both in its original form and in a piano-duet arrangement, and agreed to write an alternative finale. The greatest music is not autobiographical except in a very indirect sense, but when Beethoven completed the new movement at Gneixendorf in the late autumn of 1826 he had followed Op. 130 with his two last works, Op. 131 and Op. 135, and could not return to the Jacob-like wrestling that had attained the blessing of the *Grosse Fuge*'s coda. The meaning of any musical composition can only be built up cumulatively as time elapses; at the end of Op. 130 the variety of the five movements before the fugue is felt, in retrospect, as a sequence of which the pattern is hidden until the finale.

The necessity of the fugue is not predictable, and indeed necessity is not a valid concept, for the final shape of any work is at the command of its composer. If the 'Large Fugue' had never existed, the sonata-rondo that took its place would have been accepted as the completion of a sublime Divertimento, the true and only successor to Mozart's K.563. It has few features in common with the fugue, though the octave G at the beginning arises from the last chord of the Cavatina, as does the unison G of the Overtura. Further, the first main episode, with its exquisite continually expanding melody, is in A flat, the key of the second fugue. Otherwise, apart from the formidable unison passage in the middle of the movement, this admirable piece provides a successor to the finale of Op. 59 no. 1 with such typical late-Beethoven touches as the overlapping of phrases in the theme when it returns at the end of the A flat episode.

Op. 131 in C ♯ minor

Of the five quartets two, not three, as is sometimes said, stand apart from the others. Op. 132 belongs essentially to the classical scheme, for the brief *Alla marcia* and recitative do not really disturb the four-movement plan of sonata-form *Allegro,* scherzo and trio, variation slow movement, and rondo-style finale. Considering Opp. 130 and 131 as raising to sublimity the eighteenth-century divertimento, we note that the C sharp minor work, which Beethoven thought his greatest, is the furthest removed of all from the tradi-

tional sequence of movements; both are finale-compositions, like
the Third, Fifth and Ninth Symphonies, but whereas Op. 130 ex-
tends the four-movement plan by inserting extra movements, Op.
131 abandons it altogether. Strangely enough, the only precedent
for a sonata-type work with its true sonata movement reserved for
finale is also in C sharp minor – the piano sonata Op. 27 no. 2.

In all Beethoven's instrumental fugues, the problem with which
he wrestled was one of movement. In using fugue to make a finale
he had to build up harmonic tensions in a way alien to the Bach
fugue which nevertheless was the only possible model; however,
when he decided to begin Op. 131 with a fugue the problem van-
ished. A fugal exposition, on a slow subject, will by its nature sound
like an introduction, and if, as here, the whole fugue is to lead,
without ending, to the next movement, there is no need for a
climactic coda.

The theme of the C sharp minor fugue, from which the whole
work grew, is suggested (as a totally private joke we must suppose)
in the trio of the second movement of Op. 132.

Ex. 33

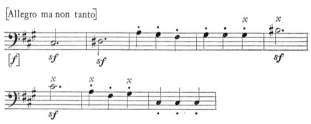

At the end of 1825 a sketch of the theme appears in a conversation
book, and some other early versions show that Beethoven proposed
a real, not a tonal, answer. A tonal answer, broadly speaking, is one
in which tonic is answered by dominant and vice versa, whereas a
real answer is a literal transposition by a fifth upwards (or, of
course, a fourth downwards). The circumstances in which one or
the other seems called for are not discernible by rule-of-thumb,
though much discussed by theorists. Clearly, subjects beginning
with the tonic will have identical first notes in the answer, whether
it is real or tonal, but where the first note is the dominant a literal
answer would begin on the main supertonic, with the effect of a
non sequitur. Accordingly Beethoven starts his answer with the 'tonal'

reply C sharp for G sharp, but continues with a literally transposed statement. This obeys the tonal rule by substituting tonic for dominant in the third and fourth bars of the theme but does allow for the tonal answer to the C sharp in the first complete bar. In effect the whole answer is on the subdominant i.e. in F sharp minor. This opening to the exposition determines a feature of the whole great design of the quartet. The first phrase in its subdominant position (this is the probable source of the inspiration) replaces the semitone above the dominant A→G sharp not by the colourless E→D sharp (the 'real' answer) but by the intense 'Neapolitan' inflection made by the semitone above the tonic, D *natural* →C sharp, its true, as distinct from 'real', equivalent.

As already remarked, there is no such thing as fugue-form. Beethoven does not even call this movement a fugue; had he given it a title he might have preferred to call it Ricercar, after the one in Bach's *Musical Offering* which he surely must have known, judging from his interest in Kirnberger, whose works he possessed in six volumes and which included resolutions of Bach's canons. Both pieces begin with a strictly fugal exposition, then expand in episodes so compelling that the subject scarcely maintains its place as the principal topic of discourse. It may or may not be coincidental that Beethoven adopts a scheme very like Bach's in that, after the exposition, a considerable episode develops and the delayed next entry of the subject is in a middle voice. In both these examples of a free fugal style in its highest development, entries of the subject are spaced widely enough to remove the assertiveness of expository argument from fugue, an element not always acceptable in some even of Bach's less inspired compositions. (The stretto fugues in the *Art of Fugue* are working models for demonstration purposes.) Beethoven's subject, incidentally, shows a close resemblance to that of the second Kyrie in Bach's B minor Mass, reaching virtual identity of rhythm when we remember how a number of Beethoven themes acquired an upbeat at a second stage of drafting. The letter (15 October 1810) in which Beethoven asks Breitkopf for J. Sebastian Bach's Mass and quotes the bass of the Crucifixus is well known. A publication of the complete Mass was announced by Simrock (1818): although the issue was long delayed Beethoven could have known the Kyrie and Gloria from the Nägeli edition of 1810. However, in this opening movement of Op. 131 Beethoven goes back to an earlier polyphony than Bach's. The canonic episode beginning in bar 65 has the remote beauty of masters even before Palestrina – Josquin or, earlier still, Ockeghem or Dufay. The notion that Beethoven knew their music is not merely fanciful. At the very time when he was working on the libretto of *Leonore,* Joseph Sonnleithner was preparing an edition of Renaissance choral music including some ten pieces by Josquin. It would be astonishing if he had not shown these to Beethoven, whose interest in early music must have been known to his colleagues. The rising sequence that follows the entry of the diminished subject in bar 53 (note the intensity of the twofold sequences in bass and treble here) is persistent to a degree scarcely to be found in any classical model, but by no means uncommon in Obrecht! When the subject appears in the treble over the beginning of the bass augmentation (bars 98–9) the very strong effect of the D *sharp* is not merely rhetorical, grand though it is as rhetoric. It turns the subdominant answer into a powerfully tonic version of the theme at a stage where the usual subdominant colour at the beginning of a coda would have no force after its prominence in the exposition.

This contradiction of the 'Neapolitan' semitone enhances the insistence on such inflections in the coda, e.g. the G natural in the augmented subject (bar 107) and the D naturals that follow (bar 112 bass, 113–15 treble).

When the bare octave that ends the 'fugue' rises yet again from C sharp to D, it needs only the F sharp in the viola to turn D into a key, with a tonic pedal in octaves beneath the melody, with its faint echo of the finale theme in Mozart's G minor quintet. Notice how the tune emphasises – the verb is too crude for such delicate suggestion – the leading note, making a converse of the stressed D→C♯ of the first movement. As the first phrase of the melody expands in the continuous variation typical of late Beethoven, it arrives at a chord of C♯ major of which the bass is concealed by the

figure | 𝄽 ♪ ♩ ♪ |, a subtle reminder that this D major is a flat supertonic in a work which has begun in what is to be its main key. The solidity of the whole tonal structure depends on the listener's acceptance of C♯ minor as a main tonic to which the music must eventually return, as all other keys are transitional – D major, F sharp minor, A major, E major, G sharp minor. By interposing the brief declamatory interlude between the *Allegro* and the central variations Beethoven avoids the too obvious key-sequence of fifths D-A-E.

This makes the impression of a perfectly lucid dialogue which says something evidently true and valuable in an unknown tongue. Its last bar carries in the bass a reference to the semitonal inflection, this time E-F *natural*.

Like all the last quartets except for Op. 130 which is in every respect unique, Op. 131 has variations for a centre. Much has been written of Beethoven's preoccupation in his later years with variation form, and little useful can be added. When action gives place to contemplation a set of variations seems the natural resource for a composer who intends a 'still centre' for a major work, where tension and contrast can be banished by a single theme that remains in its home key, or if it does change key, does so with no hint of drama. The sketch for the melody in its more or less final shape divides it between two octaves, but without showing whether this implied a division between the two violins. This alternation, without change of octave, is scarcely audible, but for the repetition of the strain the sketch form is adopted. In the second half of the melody the first violin prevails, having the whole of the first statement and all but the first two bars of the repeat. There is a mystery here as deep as the *Phoenix and the Turtle*.

'Reason in it selfe confounded
Saw Division grow together
To themselves yet either neither,
Simple were so well compounded.'

To write a canon 'three in one' was an obvious Renaissance symbol for the Trinity. Beethoven's 'Hymn of Heavenly Beauty' has no such mathematics, only poetics to account for the making of such melody out of two voices merged into one. The tonal texture is of marvellous simplicity and euphony. Much nonsense has been written about Beethoven's indifference to the medium he used to convey his musical thought, and the late quartets, because they are so obviously works of high distinction, have been described as 'abstract', soaring above mundane considerations of tone-colour or even effectiveness. In the same way Bach's *Art of Fugue,* nearly all of it carefully laid out to be playable on a keyboard, is still called 'purely musical thought' conceived with no medium in the composer's mind.

The absurdity of such views reveals itself if we compare the slow movements of the last quartets, noting how each theme has the individual string texture appropriate to its character. The stillness

of contemplation in Op. 127, with motion scarcely perceptible except in the violin at the beginning of the theme, the austere note-
against-note counterpoint of the modal opening in Op. 132, the
fantastic elaboration of decorative figures in all four parts in the
Andante of Op. 130 – each of these scores the string quartet in its
own way. In the Op. 131 *Andante* the pizzicato bass and long-held
pedal notes of the viola make a background of radiant depth and
warmth. When the first strain (the tune is a tribute to Haydn's
beatified homeliness, e.g. in *his* last quartet) is repeated, the changed
scoring is a marvel of the deaf composer's aural imagination, with
double-stopping, arco for the viola and – even more visionary – pizzicato in the bass, comparable only with the drum fifth B flat-F in the
slow movement of the Ninth Symphony. The second strain is no
less imaginatively scored; the tenths of the violins become even
richer when replaced in the repeat by second violin and viola. The
necessity of moving the pedal notes given to the viola produces a
redistribution of parts worthy of the closest scrutiny.

With its symmetrical binary structure of eight-bar phrases, the
theme and its strictly corresponding variations show Beethoven as
a reactionary scarcely less interested in 'progress' than Bach. The
understanding of his last works has been hindered by the flimsily
based supposition that he was breaking the bonds of classical tradition and exploring new formal possibilities. The truth is that the
aesthetic virtues of his predecessors found in late Beethoven their
final glorification. What makes this music hard to understand is the
remoteness from common experience of its ethos, not its 'form'.
Thus in these variations, both the harmonic scheme – itself of great
simplicity – and the phrase-structure are easily recognisable in
every variation. Because he makes the main outline so plain, Beethoven is able to indulge his fantasy in endless subtleties of detail.
Notice how, for instance, in the first variation (Ex. 34 overleaf)
the melody of the theme is preserved by alternate half-phrases in
violin and viola, the process being reversed at the repeat.

Variation II is a simplified version of the equivalent section in Op.
127 (also Variation II), but Variation III, though strictly based on
the theme, propounds an enigma in a musical speech as lucid as
could be conceived. The piece is marked *lusinghiero* (who is coaxing
whom?) – but this hint at a meaning evidently applies only to the
first half, where the theme is very precisely represented by a canonic
dialogue of the rarest beauty, with the gentle insistence inherent in

Ex. 34

bars 32 ff.
Andante ma non troppo e molto cantabile

canon at the second. Two models, both familiar to Beethoven, are the sixth of Bach's Goldberg Variations and the Recordare in Mozart's *Requiem,* and these must surely have suggested the passage in the *Missa Solemnis* of which the quartet variation is so clearly a reminiscence. The reference to the Benedictus is almost direct quotation,

Ex. 35

Benedictus   Mass in D

so close as to make untenable suggestions that Beethoven intended some joke at the expense of school-counterpoint, though the beauty of the music here should be proof against such inadequate responses.

In the second half of this variation the canonic idea is applied to purposes of clear-cut dissonance in extreme contrast with the first part. The subject is developed from a figure in the latter part of the theme, and is not a free episode. The fourth variation reverses the mood-sequence by placing the elusive remote humour in the first half, with its wilfully ineffective pizzicati: these are absent from the second half, where exchange of phrases based on the beginning of the theme alternates with sustained melody against rising scales as celestial as those at the end of 'Et vitam venturi' in the *Missa Solemnis*. The technique of double variation, used consistently throughout these variations, gives prominence to this scale-figure when the first violin's semiquavers rise from its lowest G sharp to the E more than two-and-a-half octaves above.

The finale of Op. 74 had shown how well a simplification of a variation-theme could contrast with more orthodox treatment, and the penultimate complete variation in Op. 131 (other partial variations belong to the coda) conceals both melody and pulse in overlapping chords. However, harmonic structure and phrase length are faithfully preserved and fragments of the original melody emerge momentarily, e.g. at the beginning of the second half. Beethoven's precision and accuracy were as old-fashioned in 1825 as Bach's canons in the 1740s; these qualities were equally indispensible in both, for a casual quasi-variation (see Mendelssohn) is as perishable, once seen through, as a pseudo-fugue or canon. To depart from the basic specification is to break the contract, and the results do not remain interesting. (See Ex. 36 overleaf.)

At first the *Adagio*, which makes a centre to the whole work, is a strict variation, with the twice 8-bar structure observed and the essentials of the original melody transformed into more deeply

Ex. 36

expressive equivalents. For instance, the theme's rise through an octave in its first section, to subside through the mild chromaticism of secondary sevenths alternating D sharp with D natural, is precisely 'realised' in the variation. When the strain is repeated, itself varied as we have come to expect (the only exception is the second half of Var. V), the strange bass figure that is to break up all this calm is, for the moment, rebuked into silence as the melody floats high above it, the beauty of its descent enhanced by the tenths between first violin and viola. However, Beethoven's special marking *cantabile* is withheld and the disruptive figure, similarly dismissed in the second half, returns to stay. There is nothing menacing or sinister about this ostinato; like other things in this work, it is completely lucid and mysterious beyond understanding, though when the scherzo begins its first bar might be traced back to the last section of the variation when, for some reason (but what?) Beethoven finally deletes the crotchet so that

The rest is coda; in all the late variation-sets Beethoven expands thematic figures beyond the rhythmic structure given by the theme, thus making plain the point of departure for a peroration of some kind, though not for any rhetorical climax. The especial problem of the coda in variations arises from the unvarying tonality of the classical scheme. Nothing much can be made out of the reassertion of a tonic that has never ceased to be present. In Op. 131 a further complication arises from the continuous form of the work itself. How is a developing tonal plan running through a sequence of seven movements to contain, as centrepiece, a variation-set that never leaves its own key which is not the main tonic? Clearly the coda, for once, will have to leave the key of the movement. So, after a bridge-passage with elements of recitative (it is not free, but may be traced to the harmonic outline of the theme), the first half of the original melody sets out cheerfully in the wrong key, *Allegretto* in C major. It hurries, seized by a feeling of insecurity, until it discovers that the way home is easy, all that is needed being to turn E F E into E F *sharp* E; this done, it repeats the beginning of the melody, to continue almost to the end of the first strain, in a texture both neat and gaudy, with chains of trills around the tune itself, while the cello pretends to be some kind of unknown continuo instrument. For a second time the violin trill shifts from C sharp to C natural, and the C major interlude is repeated, now in F. In this less remote key there is no need to repeat the E F E – now A B flat A – with the changed inflection; the note insisted on is the tonic of the movement, and the last figure of the theme appears in its proper key, but confidence has been lost and it cannot get beyond its own dominant without repeating itself nervously and pausing for reflection.

The last four bars were written out in score twelve times in Beethoven's tireless search for perfection. The word *semplice* against the pause before the scherzo is presumably a warning to the leader not to improvise at this point!

The tonal sequence of the quartet leads readily enough to E major, though there is a nice point of relatedness made by the harmonisation of the very direct folk-type theme. By making it turn to the mediant *major* Beethoven, through its numerous repetitions, uses the most characteristic feature of this very simple tune to remind us that C sharp is the tonic of the work. (The mediant of E major, that is to say G sharp, when major is also the dominant chord of C sharp [minor].)

Though entirely free from the grim energy of the Bagatelle in B minor, Op. 126 no. 4, this *Presto* is nearer to it than to any normal scherzo. (The scherzo of the Sonata Op. 31 no. 3 though, like the present movement in duple time, takes the place of a slow movement.) Its engaging second theme, even more elementary than the first in its self-repeating phrase-pattern, refers back over a quarter of a century to Op. 18 no. 2.

Ex. 37

This very plain connection may give plausibility to the resemblance between the variation theme and the slow movement of Op. 18 no. 3. It would not be surprising if Beethoven in returning to the Greek 'nothing-too-much' ideal of Haydn and Mozart should have recollected his own earlier music.

For all its plain speech the *Presto* shows the hand of the master-magician everywhere, whether in its rhythmic subtleties that combine epigrammatic wit with the continuous development of phrase-structure essential to sonata, or in the highly original way in which the themes are connected. Where everything seems so innocent the *sul ponticello* (the weird toneless rustling is made by placing the bow almost on the bridge) strikes a chill note, maintained through the final crescendo with its horn figure to the grim gesture of the octave G sharps. This is the turning-point of the work. So far the series of marvellously lucid inventions has moved in a world beyond the extremes of sensibility, as though the free creativeness of the intellect could be sovereign against the limitations of common experience.

Beethoven offers neither escape into the fantasies of dream-fulfilment nor the bogus consolations of pseudo-Oriental mysticism. It is the brilliantly gifted introverts of the second rank who, swaying on, or over, the edge of sanity, exalt their art into a key to the universe. One thinks of Mallarmé, Scriabin – some might say, even of Wagner. The appalling miseries and squalors of Beethoven's life in his last years did not drive him to musical autobiography, nor did he collapse into the kind of religious conversion that replaces or reinforces the consolation of drink or drugs. His magnificent sanity and mundane common sense never left him, and the penultimate movement of Op. 131 hints at tragedy with a Mozartian quietness even more moving than the utterly genuine eloquence of the heartbroken speech of the Cavatina in Op. 130. Whether or not Fétis was right in saying the melody was derived from an old French song is unimportant (it has also been associated with *Kol Nidrei*): what is noteworthy is that such a notion was possible. (The existence of sketches for a theme proves nothing concerning its originality. A composer may gradually remember something he had heard in another man's work.) Unlike the Cavatina which, as its name implies, has something of a deliberately pathetic monologue, this brief *Adagio* is 'true as truth's simplicity'. As transition to a tragic finale it makes the recitativo in Op. 132 seem very 'stagey' indeed.

In its persistent dotted rhythm the Op. 131 finale has an obvious resemblance to that of Op. 59 no. 2. It is remarkable that an early sketch in 6/8 begins in F sharp minor and remains there as far as the notes run, at which point Beethoven writes 'später nach Cis moll', i.e. the movement was to begin out of its key in a far more emphatic way than the E minor finale, where the tonal ambiguity is less marked than is commonly stated.

What is significant of the overall scheme of Op. 131 is the persistence, in this particular sketch, of the note D natural. Beethoven does not put a key signature, but assumes four sharps and writes naturals before the Ds. Presumably the motivation of this proposed opening in the subdominant was to relate first and last movements by beginning the finale in the key implied by the 'answer' in the fugal exposition. Such a plan was abandoned for one more deeply involved in the thematic structure of the whole work, and the finale begins with the formula-like assertion of tonic and dominant in the

C sharp minor now to be reasserted as the main tonic of a work in which it has scarcely featured. Having noted a structural resemblance between the first movement of Op. 131 and the six-part Ricercar in Bach's *Musical Offering*, I venture to suggest that the same work provides a possible origin for this first theme in the finale.

Ex. 38

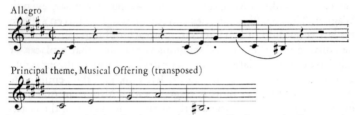

The sequel to this beginning contains an allusion to the fugue subject of the first movement which, like certain procedures in the *Grosse Fuge,* suggests the ancient device of isorhythm. The melody is changed and with it, of course, the harmonic structure, but the note values are identical (in diminution). A 'second subject', in E major, is brief, for reasons apparent later, but its extraordinary eloquence gives it great weight in the tonal scheme.

The development, in contrast to most of Beethoven's from his earliest works onwards, is not exploratory in matters of key. Sonata movements that do not repeat the exposition will normally begin developments by a part-reprise of the first theme in the tonic – a procedure followed by Brahms in his Fourth Symphony. Beethoven varies it here by repeating as much as the opening fifteen bars, but in the subdominant. This, rather than the sketch for the main theme mentioned, is the balancing feature to the subdominant of the fugue exposition; similarly the move through B minor suggests (see bars 117–25) the 'Neapolitan' D major of the second movement. In this part of the movement the long scale-figure derived from the second subject (bars 56–7) becomes important.

The master who had earlier found alternatives to classical conventions now restores them. The development, as terse and concentrated as Mozart's in, say, the 'Prague' symphony, finds itself momentarily in D major again (after bar 130) and, so compelling is the Neapolitan idea, thence in the home tonic, too soon for the reprise. The bass settles on G sharp with the rhythm of the first bars ♫ ♩ and the most conventional device at such a point is used as never before. This dominant preparation, in three-bar phrases (note the very Beethovenish shortening of note values in the bass), leads to a broadened version of the opening with such force that the string quartet, purely in terms of its own technique, becomes as powerful as an orchestra.

The allusion to the fugue does not now lead immediately to the second subject but to a wonderful quiet expansion of the iambic rhythm, with an ironical pathos found, in less subtle expression, in the scherzo of Op. 95. Beethoven's favourite crescendo to a sudden *p* was never more touching than in the appearance of the awaited theme in the inevitable yet astonishing D major.

As early as the piano sonata Op. 10 no. 1 (first movt) Beethoven had recapitulated his second subject in a key other than the tonic. Years later, in the finale of the piano trio Op. 70 no. 2, a double recapitulation was the outcome of an unusual key-structure which had begun with the exposition.[1] In Op. 131 there is nothing to lead us to expect the flat supertonic, for the theme had appeared quite normally in the exposition, in the relative major. Now its latter phrases expand, with a passing reference to the main theme deprived of its harshness (viola, bars 237 and 241) as D major moves quietly to C sharp *major* for the counterstatement. For tragic irony this parallels the tonic major in the first movement of the Ninth Symphony (bars 469ff.), though the crudity of verbalisation will show in any attempt to describe music on this level. The coda (notice the return of the D major element in bars 329–30 and 333–4), after a silent bar to give maximum emphasis without dynamic stress, makes a strange conflation of the whole work's first and last movement themes, with the allusion to the fugue in octaves reminiscent of the end of the *Grosse Fuge* (bars 708ff.). The last reference to the dotted rhythm, *poco adagio,* before the grand *tierce de Picardie* cadence, is Beethoven's latest evocation of the Mozart of K.491 – the coda of the finale. As Nottebohm recorded, the sketches for Op. 132 were divided from those for Op. 131 by a canon 'Freu dich des Lebens' ('Enjoy life').

Op. 135 in F major

Op. 131 was finished in July 1826, just before Beethoven was in-

[1] Tovey, *Beethoven* (Oxford, 1944), p. 109, for an admirable description.

volved in the most painful of the many afflictions of his last years, the disappearance and attempted suicide of his nephew. Certainly he completed his last quartet at Gneixendorf in the late autumn, but it was probably begun earlier, for Holz remarked in July that it would be the third in F (with Op. 18 no. 1 and Op. 59 no. 1). About the same time he was thinking about a replacement for the *Grosse Fuge*; the theme quoted by Nottebohm (II p. 524) shows that, for the time at least, he was in the mood of Blake's 'Damn braces, bless relaxes!'; two years earlier the profound theme of the variations in Op. 127 had, in the course of the sketches, insisted on appearing as a cheerfully ambling *Allegro grazioso* to be called 'La gaieté' (*sic*). Evidently Beethoven's reaction against the superhuman concentration demanded by these late works was to return, unafflicted by romantic nostalgia, to the less exacting world of his youth. We must not make rash generalisations on the basis of his last compositions, for their status as such is purely accidental. The five quartets might well have formed a marvellous interlude between the Ninth Symphony and *Missa Solemnis* and the proposed Requiem with the Tenth Symphony of which Holz claimed to have heard Beethoven play through the first movement. All that can be said is that he was pleased, in 1826, to occupy himself with music less exploratory than recreative. If, in the event, Op. 135 became a strangely individual work, this was only to be expected from a composer for whom self-conscious revivals of past styles (neo-classicism) were as unthinkable as rigid *a priori* systems.

The first movement does perhaps glance with affectionate irony at the old-style formal transition (bars 24–31), though the scrupulously prepared suspensions in the following passage are too beautiful not to sound serious. When the development combines the opening theme with the sevenths of the first transition phrase (bar 10) the twentieth century seems nearer than the eighteenth. Mozart's Emperor might have said 'Too few notes, Beethoven'. After only a few bars of this admittedly closely-worked development, a recapitulation pretends to take over in the subdominant, but we are not deceived. This ancient device was not very amusing as far back as Op. 10 no. 2, but there are new aspects of old jokes for him who has the wit to find them, and when the theme begins again in the right key (bar 84) this will not do either, and the genuine recapitulation must wait until impatience makes the gently insistent D flat of the very first bar become declamatory, almost melodramatic, in bars 100–2. By decorating the transition theme Beethoven makes it sound like a new idea (which, therefore, it is).

Ex. 39

When the coda begins like the development, but with this quaver variant instead of the original, the effect is doubly mysterious, the harmony being made ambiguous by the C sharp, D sharp, G sharp inflections (D flat, E flat, A flat?). The last felicity is the return of the main theme in B flat (as in the false reprise) to provide just the touch of subdominant needed at this late stage.

If this wonderful *Allegretto* reconciles stylistic opposites with the equanimity attributed to Chinese philosophers, the *Vivace* feigns a confusing of hawks and handsaws and is perhaps the most disquieting movement in the quartets, not because its humour is 'black', but rather on account of a suspicion that we who hear it are the object of its mockery. Which of the two non-melodies of the first eight bars is to be accepted as the theme? What is to come of the E flat that enters so 'meaningfully' but vanishes unidentified? Notice too the atrociously rough two-part writing when the opening is inverted without the benefit of the inner parts, primitive though they are. When the rest of this section settles down happily into something normal and euphonious enough for Op. 18 we recognise a continuation of the scheme of contrasts in the *Allegretto*. The conventional tonics and dominants before the double bar make the return of the E flat more disturbing than before, but the long sequences that follow the repeat are quietly exhilarating in the familiar Beethoven scherzo manner, with splendid modulations on the plan F major – G major – A major, an unclassical structure of key relations reminiscent of the first movement of the 'Pastoral' symphony.

Obviously a fourth step to B major is unthinkable, but Goethe's apprentice magician could not have been more shocked at his experiment than is the first violin when the other three players repeat over and over again the innocent little figure that had appeared unnoticed at the double bar. All that can be done is to put over this most obstinate of ostinatos a *Volksweise* based vaguely on the opening of the movement, using the open A as a kind of trampoline to keep it in the air. Like the E flat but far more noisily, this does not do anything, but simply fades away in its own time. When the 'main' section returns it cannot find its bass for the first eight bars.

Whether as minuet or scherzo the main section – trio – *da capo* scheme normally places the trio as a lighter, contrasting interlude, as indeed is evident from its designation, whether in three parts or not. Mozart, of course, had reversed these proportions, e.g. in the C major quintet, K.515, where the trio is not merely longer than the *Menuetto*, but full of the deepest Mozartian ambiguity. In Op. 135 the naïve listener would be right in hearing the movement as a continuous texture culminating in the grimly obstinate A major climax which is inescapably its most striking part and occupies nearly as much time-space as the whole 'main' scherzo.

Beethoven had only a year earlier written another *Volksweise,* also in A major and similarly revolving round the open A string. If the trio of Op. 132, *piano e dolce,* presents a version of pastoral full of poetry – remote without taint of nostalgia – the episode in the later work is about as romantic as Breughel and might be read as Beethoven's comment on the 'idiocy of rural life'. What raises it above the 'characteristic-piece' level is the subtlety of the violin solo, in rhythm as well as in melodic unpredictability, over the mindless repetitions of the harmless first bar at the beginning of the 'trio'. Perhaps it is brain-proprietor Beethoven's comment on his land-proprietor brother.

Op. 130 had integrated its extremes of varied keys and textures by gathering up everything into the *Grosse Fuge.* In Op. 135 contrast is taken to its limit in the succession of scherzo – slow movement; what connection can be felt between the wilfulness of the *Vivace* and the earnest gravity of the *Lento*? The difference is between kinds – something new to music though familiar enough in Shakespearian drama. If Beethoven had retained the earlier version of his slow movement theme as it appears in a sketch-book the change of mood would have been even more abrupt, for the opening two-bar

building-up of the D flat tonic chord was added after the theme itself had been perfected. There is an obvious parallel with the
famous extra bar at the beginning of the *Adagio* in Op. 106, but
there is no thematic reference in the quartet, nor is a link needed
between the not distant keys of F and D flat. (Beethoven could, of
course, have evaded the issue by placing his *Lento* after the first
movement.)

It is now customary to describe this 'song of repose or peace', as
Beethoven called it, in terms of a normal theme-and-variations
structure, but such is not the effect on the hearer who listens to
what the music tells him. It would be more useful to observe that
Beethoven uses a hidden variation element to give unity to a continually expanding *Gesang* (his word). The deeply pathetic *Più
lento* is concealed as variation (it is far more important to grasp
its quasi-recitativo quality) and when at the return to Tempo I the
whole theme appears in the bass, it is surely clear that Beethoven
has no intention of building a variation movement, but rather a
concentrated meditation on and around the admirably plain melody
(which is a perfect example of the type to which the Cavatina of
Op. 130 belongs, with perhaps the *Adagio* of the violin sonata Op.
96). A point worthy of notice is the vanishing, for the whole statement after the *minore* (bars 33–40), of the very expressive dynamics
that are an essential part of the design up to that point. Indeed, in-
sofar as the *minore* can be heard as variation, this is a result of the
reproduction of the crescendo – p nuance in the opening statement.
Compare, for instance, bars 7–8 with bars 24–7. When players observe Beethoven's markings the stillness of the cello melody with
its canonic violin counterpart is so impressive that the device seems
a new and important discovery, however neglected by later composers. The linear diatonic part-writing used in Op. 132 reappears
in this dialogue between cello and first violin. Has a dominant
seventh (X in Ex. 40 overleaf) ever sounded so new (since Monteverdi!) as at the beginning of this section?

Scarcely less unclassical is the texture of bars 38–41, where the
tonic falls so oddly yet convincingly. The coda, like so much in the
work, is original in its fresh approach to time-honoured procedures.
(The routine adjective is meant to be exact.) First, as the melody dissolves into brief phrases, lightened by rests, the second violin hints
at a repeated dominant. Then the bass descends in slow steps, its
long notes echoed within the pattern of the second violin's reiter-

Ex. 40
bars 33-34

ated figure. This beautiful device of concealed octaves is quite
unclassical in quartet-writing, though familiar enough in keyboard
figuration. Much has been written of the thematic allusions and
cross-references that pervade this quartet – in guises more convincing than some of the discoveries (or inventions) of modern ana-
lysts – for instance, the unmistakable though musically non-signifi-
cant connection between the slow movement and the theme of the
finale.

Ex. 41(a)

(Finale 1st subj.)
Allegro

(b)
Theme of Lento (transposed)

(c)
(Finale 2nd subj.)

The principal subject of the finale is an improved version of the theme Beethoven wrote down in April 1826 as a canon to the words 'Es muss sein, ja, es muss sein. Heraus mit dem Beutel'. This may be rendered as 'It must be, certainly it must. Put cash on the table!' Carl Holz related how one Dembscher, an amateur musician, tried to borrow the parts of Op. 130. Told that the fee would be 50 gulders, he said reluctantly, 'Wenn es sein muss!' ('If it has to be!'). Beethoven, in high good humour, immediately scribbled the canon, which is for four voices. When he came to write the quartet movement he spelt it out in capitals: DER SCHWER GEFASSTE ENT-SCHLUSS ('The hard-made decision').

Much speculation has been focused on the meaning of this superscription and of the motto later placed before the beginning of the finale itself. Admittedly the canon was inspired by a mundane incident, but how 'serious' was Beethoven's intention in the quartet movement? Such queries are not very useful, for it is not in the nature of music to make statements of intent. In the autumn of 1806 he had composed the 32 Variations (Woo 80), a piece full of the Beethovenian C minor fiery pathos, but a few years later, according to the well-known anecdote, the composer of this grand passacaglia dismissed it with 'Such stuff by me? Oh, Beethoven, what an ass you were!' The many sketches dealing with the motto question-and-answer show that the idea was not frivolous, but to ask whether it is meant seriously is as futile as to ask the same about the C minor Variations or even about a much greater work, the 'Appassionata'. What would the Beethoven of Op. 135 have said to the grand rhetorical gestures of that sonata's first and last movements, with their resounding diminished sevenths?

It is possible to take a highly sophisticated view of the fortissimo return, in the latter part of the Op. 135 finale, of the *Grave* with its anxious 'Must it be'?, and to regard it as histrionic. No one can disprove such a reading, but it is not Beethoven's way, any more than it is Shakespeare's, to mock at intensity of feeling. It is true that the dramatic language is very much of its time: both tremolo and 'affective' intervals belong to the vocabulary of early Romantic opera, and the element of non-personal statement is surely a necessary one in this unique fusion of words and music. The slightly old-fashioned air of the instrumental recitative (Beethoven had in a few years moved far from the Ninth Symphony world of communal aspiration) is emphasised by the unobtrusively subversive linear style already mentioned in connection with Op. 135. Consider the first bars of the *Allegro* ('Es muss sein'), or the frequently 'neo-classical' relations between treble and bass. It is idle to speculate about Beethoven's intentions for works after 1826, but the whole classical scheme of harmonically-based polyphony is casually undermined in Op. 135. No wonder the second *Grave* draws the cheerful 'Es *muss* sein' into its distressful unresolvable dissonances. Serious or not, there should be no mistaking the touching pathos of the now diminished fourth F-C, sadly changed to G flat-D natural.

In the coda this very subtle transformation of the cheerful reply into the pathetic question reaches its most intense expression, to be dismissed by the no less extreme heavenly levity of the pizzicato version of Ex. 41 c, itself of course a form of the affirmative motto.

Among the great composers who followed Beethoven some were to emulate the gravity and depth of his last slow movement, but none seems to have recognised the challenge of the finale of Op. 135. In the century after him, Beethoven's great middle-period works were a continued challenge and an inspiration not always felicitous, but no one before our own age seems to have recognised the possibility of recovering, through the latest Beethoven, the true Mozartian tradition by which the most serious things could, after all, be said without solemnity or portentousness.

When Chaucer's Troilus had been killed, his 'lighte goost' travelled blissfully to the seventh sphere, whence he looked down on the Earth:

> 'And at the laste,
> There he was slayn, his loking doun he caste;
> And in him-self he lough right at the wo
> Of hem that wepten for his deeth so faste.'